Aa	Bb	Cc	Dd	Ee
Ff	Gg	Hh	IiJj	Kk
Ll	Mm	Nn	Oo	Pp
Qq	Rr	Ss	Tt	Uu
Vv	Ww	Xx	Yy	Zz

A B C D E F G H I J K L M N O P Q R S T U V W X Y Z

My Fun Pic

Note to parents

This Fun Picture Dictionary has been designed to teach young children how to use a dictionary. Just like a traditional dictionary, it lists words in alphabetical order, and provides clear definitions. In addition, bright photographs illustrate every word, and an amusing caption gives a real-life example of how the word could be used. Full of interesting facts, games, and challenging questions, this is much more than just a dictionary – it's a word explorer.

Designed by Neville Graham
Edited by Jo Douglass
Photography by Richard Brown
Except: p.48, Nest (Ardea, b Trap-Lind)
p.63, Sharks (Ardea, Mark Spencer).

This book was made by Roger Priddy, Joanna Bicknell, Robert Tainsh, Jo Douglass, Louisa Beaumont, Neville Graham, Cameron Emerson-Elliott, Jo Rigg, Rebecca Clunes, Sarah Kappely, and Dan Green.

We hope you enjoy this book as much as we enjoyed making it.

Copyright © 2003 St. Martin's Press, 175 Fifth Avenue, New York, NY 10010.

Published by
priddy bicknell
A division of Macmillan Publishers Ltd

All rights reserved, including the right of reproduction in whole or in part in any form.

Manufactured in Malaysia.

between
Natasha and Rebecca are having fun playing with a beachball. Rebecca is keeping it **between** her legs and Natasha is trying to get it.

car
When Maria grows up she wants to drive a shiny red sports **car**. In the meantime, she'll have to make do with her little brother's toy **car**.

ure Dictionary

firefighters
Thank goodness. The **firefighters** have arrived and are putting out the fire with water from their hose. **Firefighters** are so brave!

itch
Nicole's cat, Millie, is scratching herself. She must have an **itch**. Maybe she has fleas. Oh no!

young
Nicole is **young**, but not as **young** as her sister Lauren, and Lauren is not as **young** as their baby brother. He's the youngest of them all.

Sheila Hanly

priddy ○ bicknell
big ideas for little people

A B C D E F G H I J K L M N O P Q R S T U V W X Y Z

Aa

about

Max is telling Maria **about** the time he caught a huge fish. But I don't think Maria believes him.

about connected with

after

Tina did a special dance in the ballet show. **After** the show, she was given a beautiful bouquet of flowers.

after following, or later than

again

Billy is a clumsy builder. He has hit his hand **again**. That's the third time this week!

again another time, or once more

alphabet

ABCDEFGHIJ
KLMNOPQRS
TUVWXYZ
abcdefghij
klmnopqrs
tuvwxyz

There are 26 letters in the **alphabet**. Do you know them all yet? Try saying the letters of the **alphabet** out loud.

alphabet the letters used for writing a language

always

Emma's hair is **always** in a mess. No matter how often she brushes it, it still looks like a big bird's nest.

always at all times

angry

When Scott gets **angry** his face scrunches up and turns bright red. Have you ever seen your face when you get **angry**?

angry feeling very annoyed

animals

Animals come in every colour, shape and size you can imagine. Prickly or furry, noisy or quiet – how would you describe this goat?

animal a living thing that can move, feel and breathe

another

The fence is finished. That's **another** job well done. Billy and Joe have **another** cup of coffee to celebrate.

another an additional one

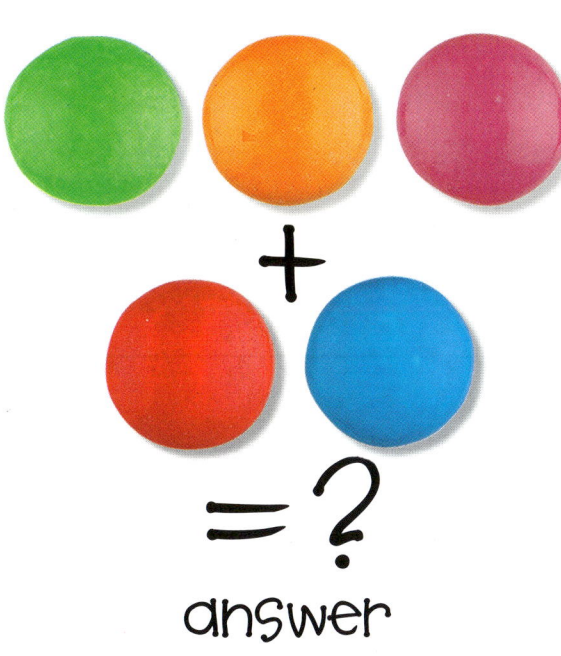

answer

Can you work out the **answer** to this puzzle? If you have three sweets and someone gives you two more, how many sweets do you have?

answer solution

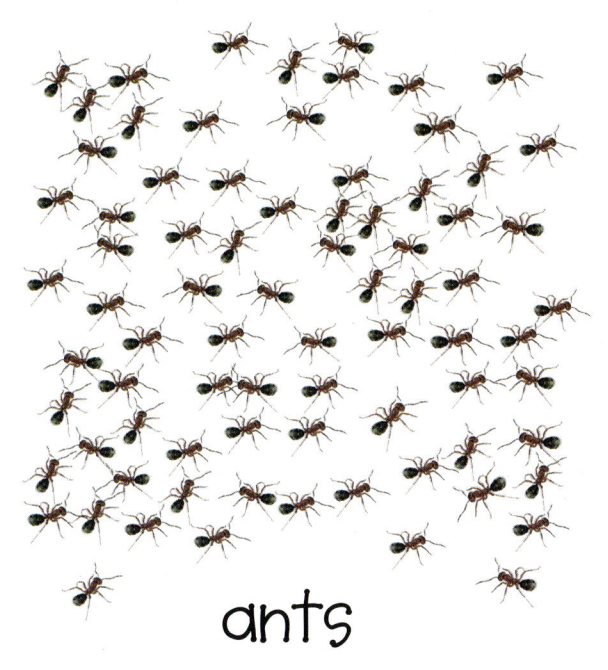

ants

Ants are everywhere. Did you know some **ants** live in nests with a million other **ants**. Imagine a million people living in your home!

ant a type of insect

apples

Apples are a crunchy, juicy treat. Do you prefer eating green **apples** or red **apples**?

apple a type of round, edible fruit

argue

Hope and Ellis often **argue** about what programme to watch on television. But they are good friends, despite the arguments.

argue to disagree or to quarrel

ask

Look, that naughty Jake has eaten a piece of his mum's chocolate cake. She told him to **ask** first.

ask to say something so you can find out an answer

astronaut

Maria would love to be an **astronaut**. She dreams about blasting off into space in a huge rocket and discovering new planets.

astronaut someone who travels into space

aunt

This is Nicole with her mum and her **aunt**. **Aunt** Joanna is her mum's sister. Has your mum or dad got a sister who is your **aunt**?

aunt the sister of your mother or father

awake

Grace heard a creaking sound outside her bedroom door. Now she's wide **awake**. What's out there? Is it a ghost?

awake not asleep

Bb

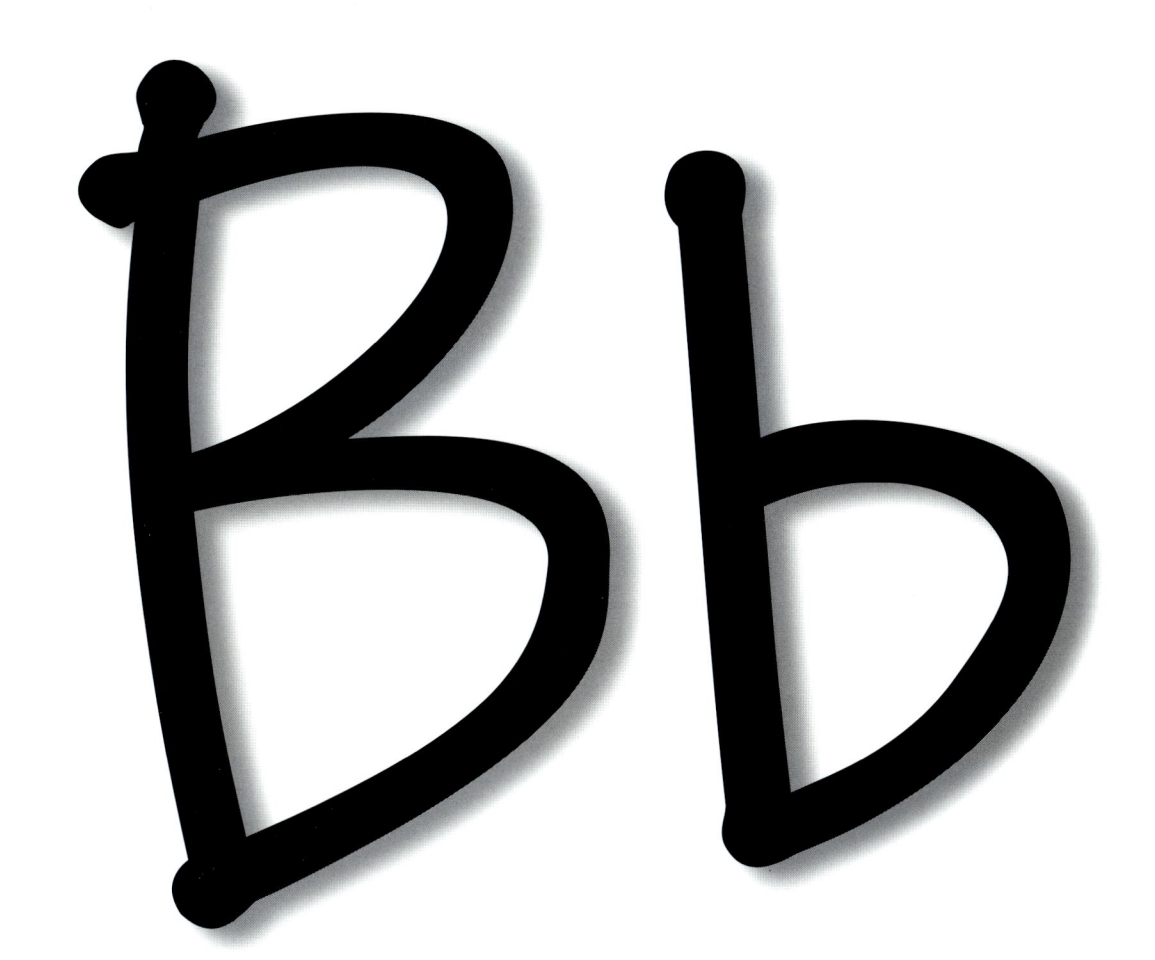

baby

This **baby** is called James. He is Nicole and Lauren's brother. Nicole thinks her **baby** brother is fun, but Lauren thinks he cries too much.

baby a very young child or animal

back

"Give that water pistol **back**!"
"No, it's mine."
"But I had it first, and now I want it **back** again."

back 1. to return
2. the side opposite the front

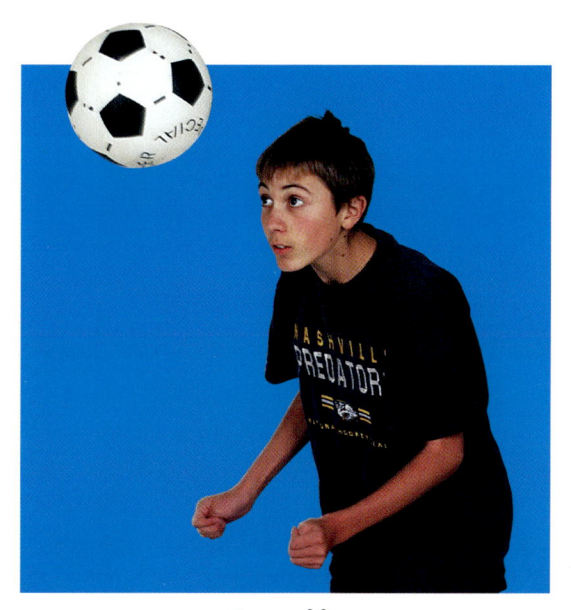

ball

One, two, three! Go on Simon, see if you can head the **ball** 20 times in a row. You're doing well!

ball a round object used as a toy or in a sport

balloon

Balloons are brilliant. I like the ones you can twist into funny shapes. I think this **balloon** is meant to look like a bug.

balloon a stretchy bag that can be blown up and used as a decoration or as a toy

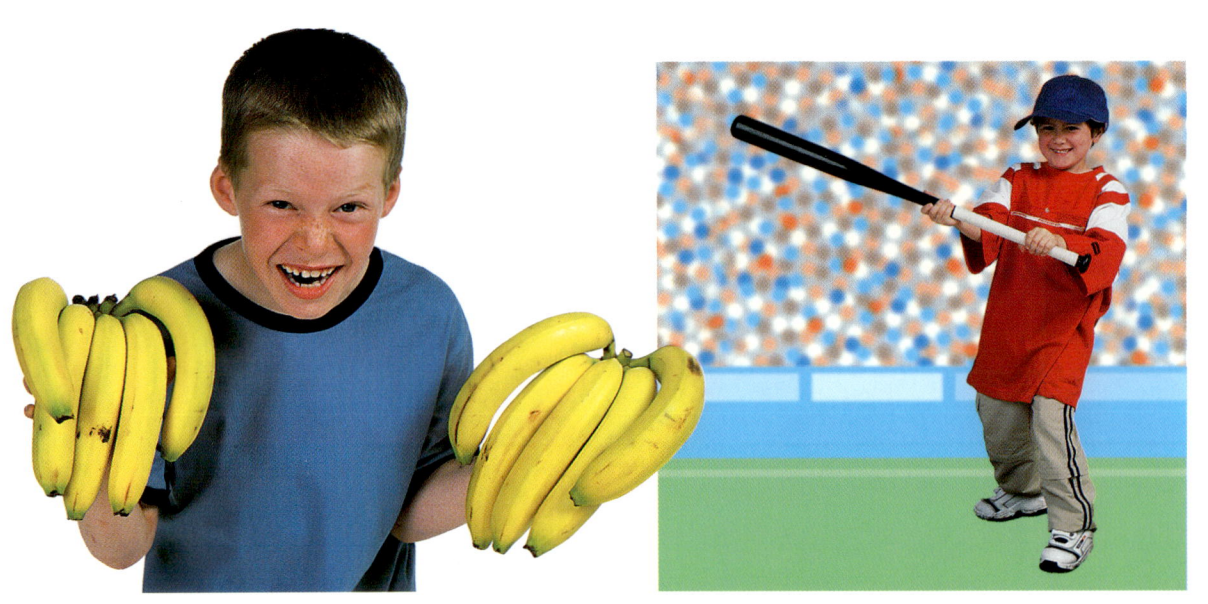

bananas

Bananas are one of my favourite snacks. **Bananas** grow in bunches called hands. It's easy to see why they are called hands, isn't it?

banana a curved yellow fruit that grows in hot countries

bat

Sam is playing baseball. It's his turn to **bat**. Are you ready, Sam? Here comes the ball. That's a big **bat** for such a little guy.

bat 1. to hit with a bat
2. a wooden stick used to hit a ball

bath

Jack is playing with his duck in the **bath**. He loves splashing around in water so much he would stay in the **bath** all day if he could.

bath a large container that is filled with water for washing oneself

beach

Natasha and Rebecca are spending the day at the **beach**. It looks like they have everything they need for a fun day out.

beach an area of sand or pebbles where the sea meets the land

bear

What does a hungry **bear** eat? Almost anything! A **bear** eats small animals, fish, insects, fruit, nuts and leaves.

bear a type of large animal with thick fur

beautiful

Princess Pam looks **beautiful** in her golden crown and royal cape. I'm sure she will be the most **beautiful** princess at the ball.

beautiful very pretty

bed

It's 8 o'clock at night and Jake is in **bed** already. I wonder if he's really asleep or just pretending. What do you think?

bed a piece of furniture for sleeping on

bee

Have you seen a **bee** flying from flower to flower? It is collecting pollen to make honey. A **bee** may visit 10,000 flowers in one day.

bee a type of winged insect that makes honey

before

Emma went to bed really late last night. Now she's too sleepy to get dressed properly. No, Emma your socks go on **before** your shoes!

before 1. earlier
2. in front of

begin

Tina is about to do the first dance in a ballet show. She takes her place on the stage and the curtain rises. Let the show **begin**!

begin to start

behind

Tina has finished her dance. Now she is hiding **behind** the curtain to watch the rest of the show.

behind 1. on the far side of
2. further back than

best

Natasha and her **best** friend, Rebecca, are eating their favourite flavours of ice cream. Which flavour ice cream do you like **best**?

best 1. favourite
2. the most

between

Natasha and Rebecca are having fun playing with a beachball. Rebecca is keeping it **between** her legs and Natasha is trying to get it.

between the space in the middle of two things

bicycle

This **bicycle** is Jessica's birthday present from her mum and dad. Can you ride a **bicycle**?

bicycle a vehicle with two wheels, pedalled by the rider

big

That's a very **big** box you've got, Max. What's that written on it? "DANGER"? I hope there isn't a **big** and dangerous animal in there!

big large

birds

Do you know what a flamingo, a chicken and a seagull have in common? They're all **birds**. Can you name any other **birds**?

bird an animal with two legs, feathers and wings

birthday

Jessica is eight today and she's having a **birthday** party with all her friends. How old will you be on your next **birthday**?

birthday the anniversary of the day someone was born

bite

Jake has taken a big **bite** out of a jam tart, but he doesn't like the jam. I'm surprised, I thought Jake would eat anything.

bite to cut into something using your teeth

blanket

This thick, fluffy **blanket** will keep you snug and cosy, even on the coldest nights.

blanket a large cloth used for keeping warm

boat

Look at this sailing **boat**. The wind is helping it to move quickly over the water. Have you ever been on a **boat** like this?

boat a floating vessel used to travel on water

bones

When Emma fell off the monkey bars, she had to have an X-ray to check if she had broken any **bones**. Poor Emma.

bones the hard parts of your body that make up your skeleton

book

Nicole is reading a story **book**, and Lauren is colouring a picture in her colouring **book**. What is your favourite **book**? Is it this one?

book sheets of paper fastened together containing words and sometimes pictures

bottles

Have you used **bottles** to make music? Fill some **bottles** with different amounts of water and then tap them with a spoon.

bottle a glass or plastic container used for holding liquid

bottom

Whizzing down the slide is fun, but you always end up at the **bottom**. Then you have to climb back up to the top to have another go.

bottom 1. the lowest part 2. the part of your body you rest on when you sit down

bowl

The porridge in the small **bowl** is not too hot and it's not too salty. I think this little girl is going to eat it all up. I wonder who she is?

bowl a rounded container used for serving food

boys

Here are some of the **boys** you've met so far in this book. Can you remember their names?

boy a male child

bread

Jake likes egg and jam on his **bread**. Emma likes peanut butter and sweets on hers. Do you like to eat weird things on **bread**?

bread a food made from flour, water and yeast, then baked

break

Lucy, be careful with those mugs! If you **break** them, your mum will be very upset.

break to separate into pieces accidentally or on purpose

breakfast

Amy usually has cereal for **breakfast**, but at weekends her mum makes her egg on toast.

breakfast the first meal of the day

brother

Sam thinks his big **brother** Matt is totally cool. Matt thinks his little **brother** Sam is pretty cool, too. So that's cool.

brother a boy who has the same parents as you

bubbles

I love blowing **bubbles**, don't you? You can see all the colours of the rainbow in them.

bubble a thin layer of liquid around a ball of air

bulldozer

Max wants to make a camp in the garden. He wishes he had a giant **bulldozer** to help clear a big space to build on.

bulldozer a vehicle used for moving earth

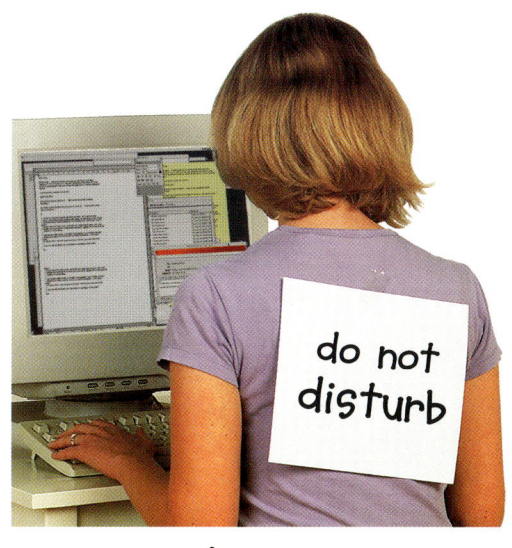

busy

Scott wants to play his music, but his mum is **busy** working. When. Scott's mum is **busy**, she does not want to be disturbed.

busy having lots of things to do

butter

If you take a bottle with some cream in it and shake it for a long, long time, the cream will turn into **butter**. Have you ever tried this?

butter a food made from cream, often spread on bread or toast

butterfly

Did you know that a **butterfly** never eats? It hasn't got any teeth, so it can't chew its food. It has to sip nectar from flowers instead.

butterfly a type of insect with pretty coloured wings

buttons

Scott's mum has asked him to turn off his music. But there are so many **buttons** on his new stereo, Scott doesn't know which one to press.

button 1. part of a machine you press to work it
2. a small, round disc used to fasten clothes

Cc

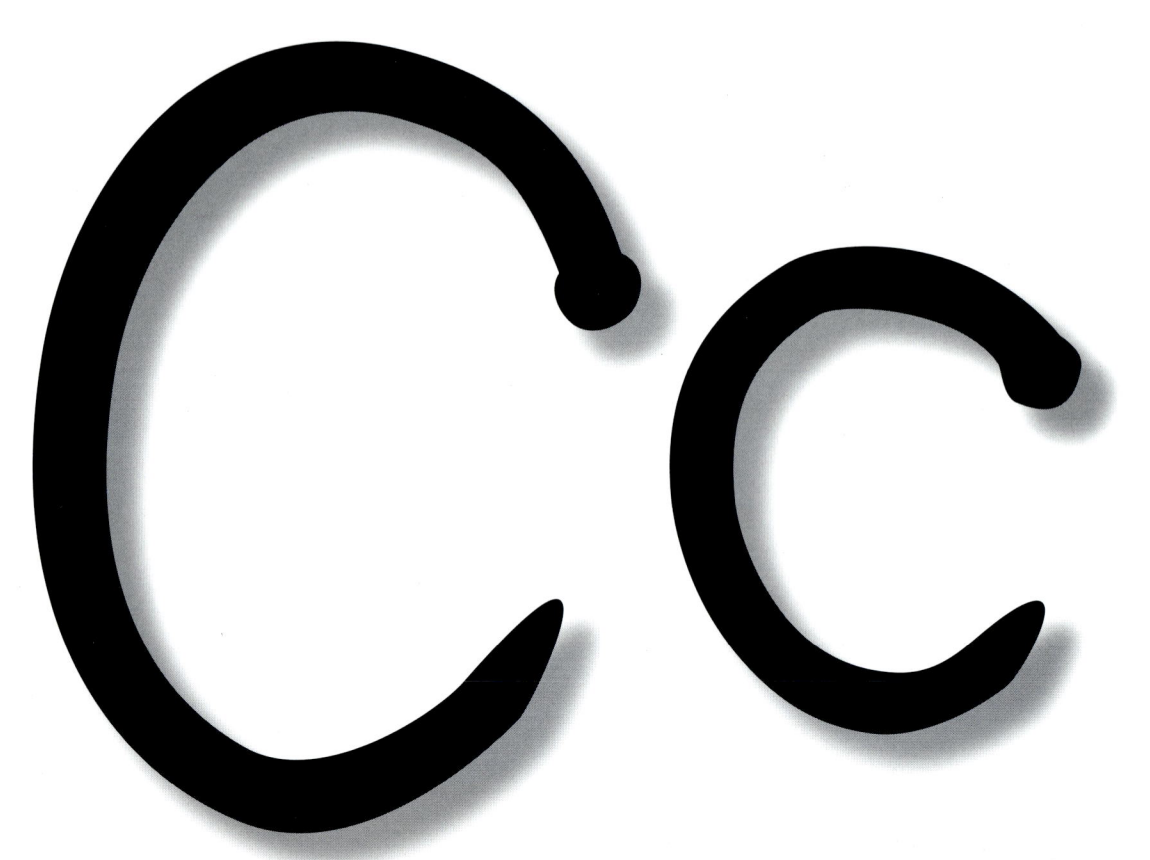

cakes

Jake likes **cakes**. Big **cakes**, small **cakes**, round **cakes**, tall **cakes**... Jake likes all **cakes**. Do you like **cakes** as much as Jake?

cake a sweet food made from flour, eggs, butter and sugar, then baked

call

"This is John from the Fire Department here, answering your **call**. What's that? A large fire? We'll be there right away."

call 1. to telephone someone
2. to shout or speak loudly to attract attention

camels

Camels live in deserts. Their humps are used to store fat. **Camels** can turn this fat into water so they can survive without drinking for long periods.

camel a large animal that can live in the desert for long periods without any water

camera

One of Jessica's birthday presents was a **camera**. Now she can take a picture of all the kids at her party. Say "cheese" everyone.

camera something you use to take photographs

can

Natasha **can** stand on her head. Rebecca **can** do it, too. **Can** you stand on your head?

can is able to

candles

Look at all the **candles** on Jessica's cake. How old do you think she is today?

candle a stick of wax with a string through it that can be burned to give light

car

When Maria grows up she wants to drive a shiny red sports **car**. In the meantime, she'll have to make do with her little brother's toy **car**.

car a vehicle for transporting people

carrots

I bet you knew that **carrots** were good for you. But did you know that eating **carrots** will actually help you to see better in the dark?

carrot an orange-coloured root vegetable

cat

This is Nicole's **cat**, Millie. Isn't she adorable? She's a tortoiseshell **cat**, but cats come in many different colours.

cat a small pet animal with soft fur and whiskers

caterpillar

When this **caterpillar** grows up it will become a beautiful butterfly. But first it needs to grow a bit bigger, so it's eating as much as it can.

caterpillar a worm-like animal that later turns into a butterfly or moth

cereal

Sam loves eating **cereal** for breakfast. That's a big bowl of **cereal** for such a little guy!

cereal a breakfast food made from oats, wheat or rice, usually eaten with milk

chair

David's dad calls this his magical **chair**. It's so comfortable that whenever he sits in it, he falls asleep immediately.

chair a seat with legs, a back and sometimes arms

cheese

Has Jake been nibbling this **cheese**? No, silly, this **cheese** is supposed to have holes in it!

cheese a food made from sheep's, goat's or cow's milk

chew

Sparky loves to **chew** things. So far she has chewed three slippers, five balls, a cushion and a tennis racket. I wonder what she'll **chew** next?

chew to grind food using your teeth and jaws

chick

This fluffy baby bird is called a **chick**. It hatched out of its egg only yesterday. Isn't it sweet?

chick a baby bird

chocolate

Jake has melted some **chocolate** to make a topping for his cake. He's going to decorate it with sweets as well!

chocolate a brown, sweet food

choose

Hope has been told that she can have a kitten. Now she has to **choose** which one she wants, but she wants to have them all!

choose to decide on something from a number of possibilities

circus

Maria wants to be a clown in the **circus**. She's learned some juggling tricks so she'll be ready next time the **circus** comes to town.

circus a travelling group of entertainers

clean

Do you like having a bath? However dirty you are, some hot water and some bubbles can make you feel all nice and **clean**.

clean not dirty

climb

Billy the builder has to **climb** up a ladder to fix a window. It's a good thing he's not scared of heights.

climb to go up

clock

Brrring! When an alarm **clock** rings, it's time to wake up. Do you have an alarm **clock** to wake you up in the morning?

clock a device for telling the time

clouds

I love looking at the **clouds** in the sky. Sometimes they look like pictures of different things. Have you ever seen funny-shaped **clouds**?

cloud millions of water droplets clinging together up in the sky

coat

It's freezing cold outside, but Steve's **coat** will keep him toasty and warm. The zip goes right up to Steve's chin to keep out the chilly breeze.

coat an item of clothing for keeping you warm outdoors

cold

This polar bear lives in the Arctic where it is always **cold**. Its coat doesn't have a zip like Steve's – the bear's coat always stays on!

cold 1. low in temperature 2. an illness where you have a sore throat and sneeze a lot

colours

This drawing of a rainbow is full of bright **colours**. Do you like using lots of different **colours** when you draw a picture?

colour the appearance of an object such as red, green, blue, yellow and so on

computer

Maria loves playing on her **computer**. She even enjoys doing her homework when she gets to do it on the **computer**.

computer a machine used to look up facts, send messages and play games

cookies

These chocolate chip **cookies** have just come out of the oven. Don't they look delicious? Yum, I can't wait to munch one!

cookie a biscuit

cousins

Nicole and Hope are **cousins**. That's because Nicole's mum and Hope's mum are sisters. Nicole and Hope are part of one big family.

cousin the child of your uncle or aunt

cow

Here's a puzzle. What goes into a **cow** is mostly green grass. And what comes out is mostly white milk. So how come milk isn't green?

cow a large female farm animal that provides milk

crab

Watch out for the big claws on this **crab**. They could give you a pretty painful pinch.

crab an animal with a hard shell, eight legs and two claws that lives in the sea

cry

Hope bumped her head and started to **cry**. Her mum gave her a big hug and kissed her head all better.

cry to shed tears because you are in pain or unhappy

cup

Sam is having a **cup** of milk, his favourite drink. That's a big **cup** for such a little guy!

cup a container with a handle, used for drinking

curly

Kate's hair is very **curly**. Sometimes she wishes she had straight hair instead of **curly** hair. Which do you prefer?

curly not straight, with lots of curls

cut

Sally has not had her hair **cut** for years. She likes it long but it does get in the way. I think she should get it **cut**. What do you think?

cut to divide something with a knife or pair of scissors

21

Dd

dance

When Tina hears music, she just has to **dance**. She loves being in ballet shows where she can **dance** in front of lots of people.

dance to move your body and feet to the rhythm of music

dark

Hey, who switched the light off? It's very **dark** in here. I can't see a thing… can you?

dark with little or no light

day

What a lovely **day**! The sky is blue and the sun is shining down on a field of pretty flowers.

day 1. the time between sunrise and sunset
2. a period of 24 hours

different

These ducks are all **different**. Or are they? Can you find two ducks that are the same?

different not the same as

dig

When Maria grows up she wants to be a gardener. She likes to **dig** in her garden and plant seeds that will grow into beautiful flowers.

dig to cut into the ground, usually with a spade or a trowel

dinner

Yuk! I wouldn't like to eat this **dinner**, would you? I expect this food looks delicious to a bird, though. I bet it's a bird's favourite **dinner**.

dinner the main meal of the day, often eaten in the evening

dinosaurs

Millions of years ago, **dinosaurs** roamed the earth. I'm glad these **dinosaurs** are only toys – they look really scary!

dinosaur a type of animal that lived millions of years ago

dirty

When Rebecca came home from playing in the mud, she was so **dirty** that only her teeth were clean!

dirty opposite of clean

doctor

When Maria grows up she'd like to be a **doctor** so she can help to make sick people well again. Today, she's practising on her bear.

doctor a person who makes sick people well again

dogs

Here's a bunch of friendly-looking **dogs**. I can see a sheepdog, a bulldog and a dalmatian. Do you know which dog is which?

dog a pet animal that has four legs and a tail and that can bark

23

door

This is the **door** to Max's bedroom. I wonder what he's got hidden behind that **door** that he doesn't want anyone to see?

door something that you open or close when you enter or leave a building or a room

down

John is sliding **down** the pole at the fire station. He is hurrying to help put out the fire.

down 1. to move to a lower place
2. the opposite of up

dress

Princess Pam is ready for the ball. She has put on her favourite **dress** and her golden crown. Doesn't she look great?

dress 1. a skirt and top in one
2. to put on clothes

drink

Camels can go for days without a **drink** of water, but we need to **drink** about eight glasses of water a day to stay healthy.

drink 1. a wholesome liquid
2. to swallow liquid

dry

After a bath, there's nothing better than snuggling into a thick, fluffy towel to get all nice and **dry** again. This baby thinks so, too!

dry opposite of wet

duck

Why does a **duck** walk on two legs and say "quack, quack"? Because if it had four legs and said "woof, woof" it would be a dog!

duck 1. a type of bird that lives on or near water
2. to crouch down to avoid something

Ee

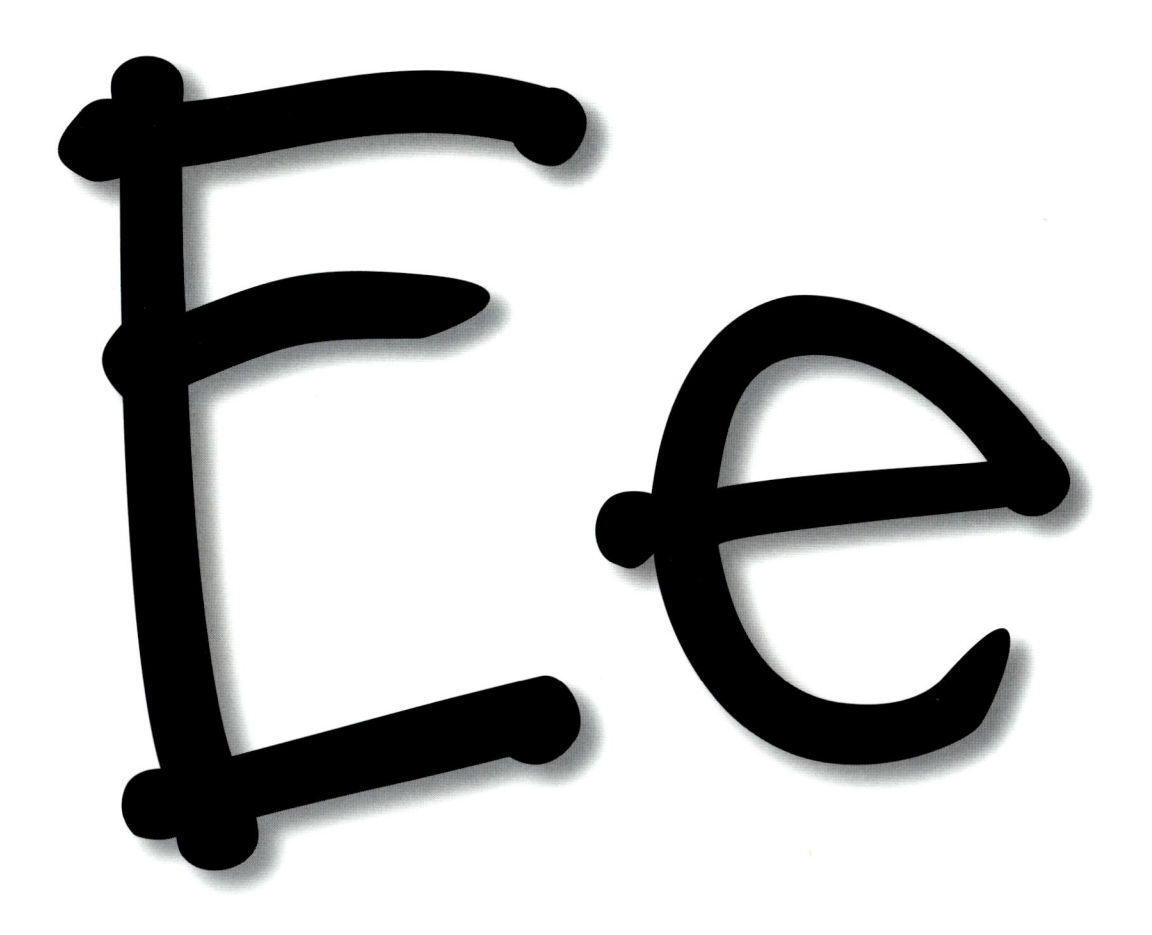

each

These children have **each** got a new pet. Can you figure out which pet belongs to which child?

each every

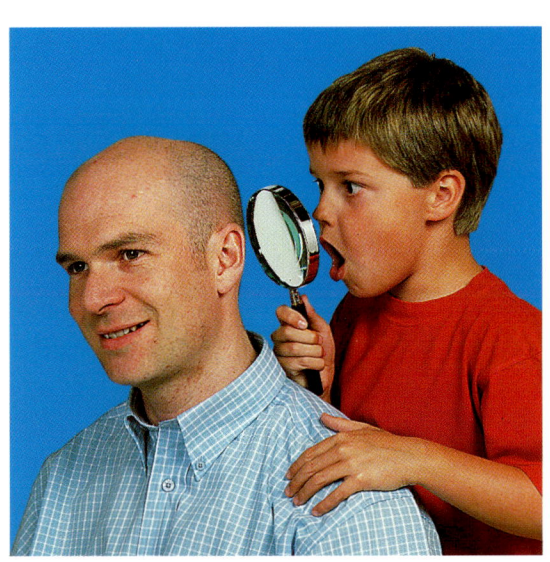

ear

Did you know that most of your **ear** is actually inside your head? You can't see it though, David, not even with a magnifying glass.

ear the part of the body that you hear with

eat

Helen would **eat** a hamburger for every meal if she could. But she knows she needs to **eat** lots of different foods to keep healthy.

eat to chew and swallow food

egg

What a funny looking face! This **egg** looks like it needs ears and some hair. Have you ever decorated a hard-boiled **egg**?

egg an oval object with a shell laid by a female bird, often eaten as a food

A B C D E F G H I J K L M N O P Q R S T U V W X Y Z

elephant

This little baby **elephant** lives with its mother. It loves to splash in the mud on the banks of a river.

elephant a very large animal with big ears and a long nose called a trunk

empty

David is feeling hungry. He wants a biscuit, but when he goes to the jar he finds it is **empty**. Who has eaten all the biscuits?

empty with nothing inside

end

Lauren is enjoying the story her mum is reading so much that she never wants to get to the **end**. Do you ever have that feeling about a book?

end the completion of something

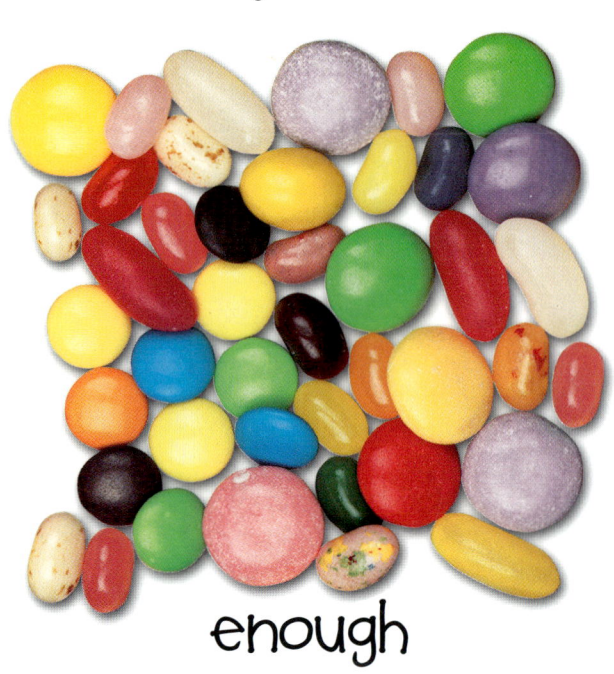

enough

What a lot of sweets! I think there are **enough** sweets for every child at Jessica's party, don't you?

enough as many as necessary

explore

When Maria grows up, she wants to **explore** the rainforest and find new plants. Meanwhile, she's happy to **explore** her back garden.

explore to go to a place and find out things about it

eyes

This frog has funny **eyes**. I wonder if the world looks yellow when you see it through yellow **eyes**?

eye a part of the body used for seeing

Ff

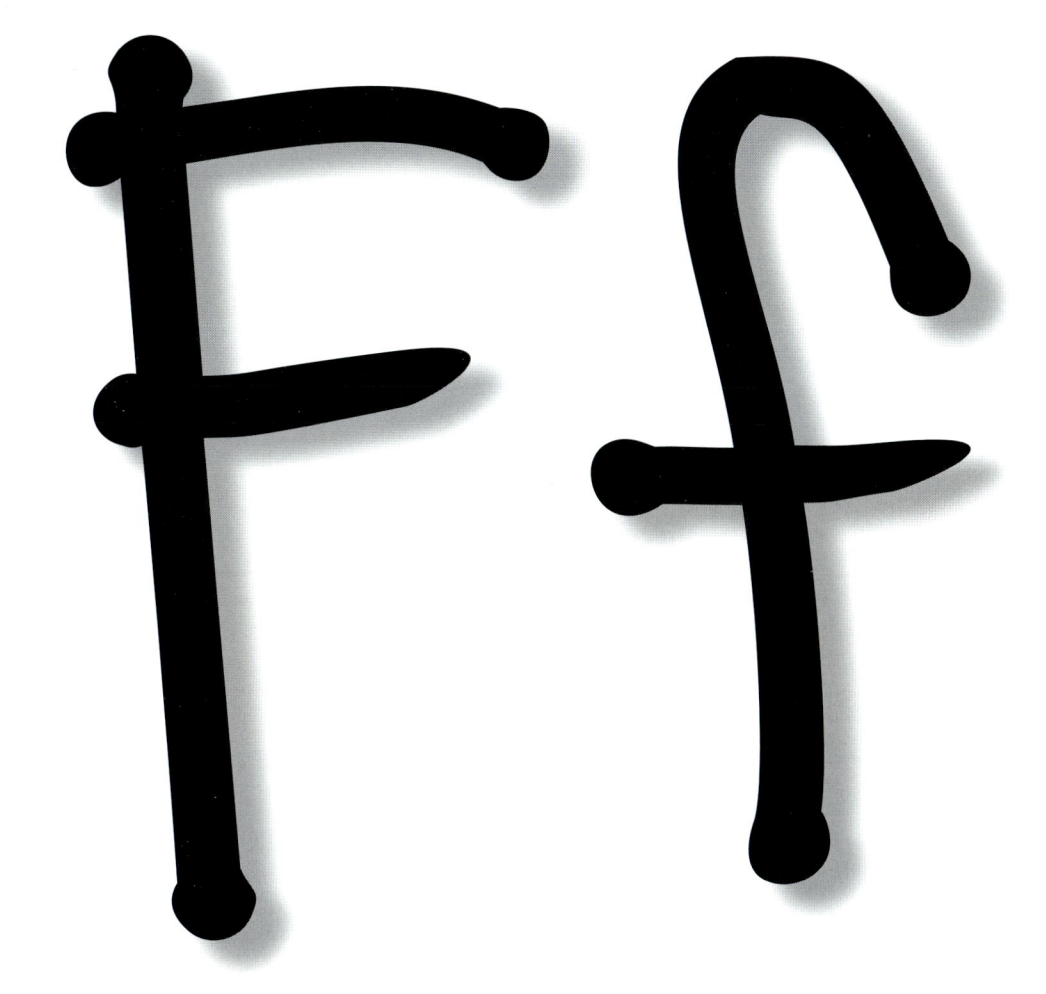

face

Two eyes, a nose and a mouth make a **face**. But all of our faces are different — even if you are an identical twin!

face the front part of the head containing the eyes, nose and mouth

fairy

This pretty little **fairy** lives in a flower. She eats only honey and she drinks out of an acorn cup.

fairy a tiny, imaginary person with magical powers and wings

fall

Scott was balancing on a wall when he slipped and hurt his knee. Poor Scott, that was a nasty **fall**.

fall to drop to the ground

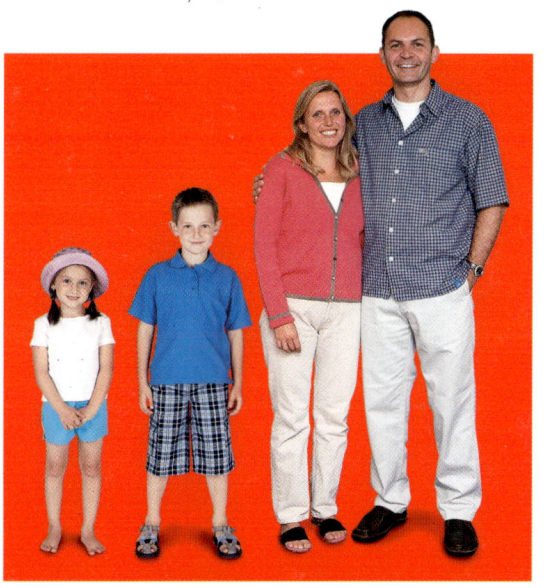

family

This **family** is made up of a mum, a dad and their daughter and son. Who's in your **family**?

family the people you are related to

fast

Look at how **fast** this gazelle is moving. I wish I could run this **fast**. But I only have two legs and a gazelle has four.

fast to move very quickly

fat

Sparky has been eating too many treats and she's getting **fat**. Nicole takes her for an extra walk to help her lose weight. Come on, Sparky!

fat having a thick body

father

David's **father** is lots of fun. No-one can make David laugh as much as his **father** can.

father your male parent

favourite

Matt's **favourite** sport is baseball. It's Sam's **favourite**, too. What's your all-time **favourite** sport?

favourite something you like the most

feather

David's dad said he was so surprised, you could have knocked him down with a **feather**. David can't imagine a bird with a **feather** that big.

feather the things attached to a bird's skin that help it to keep warm and to fly

feet

When Tina dances, she wears special soft shoes on her **feet**. They are tied on firmly with ribbons so they won't slip off her **feet**.

feet the parts of the legs below your ankles that allow you to stand, walk and dance

fence
Grace has kicked her ball over the **fence**. How do you think she'll get it back again?

fence a barrier around a garden or a field

find
Little Bo Peep has lost her sheep, and doesn't know where to **find** them. Can you help Bo Peep **find** her sheep?

find to locate something that has been lost

finger
Scott has put his **finger** in his mouth and is using it to make a loud "popping" noise. Can you make a noise like this?

finger one of the thin, jointed parts of the body at the end of a hand

fire
The **fire** chief is the first one to arrive at the **fire**. "Fire! Fire! Please keep away so you don't get hurt!" he shouts to people passing by.

fire something that burns and gives off heat, flames and smoke

firefighters
Thank goodness. The **firefighters** have arrived and are putting out the fire with water from their hose. **Firefighters** are so brave!

firefighter a person who puts out fires

first
Jessica's friends have given her lots of fabulous gifts for her birthday. Which present should she open **first**?

first the earliest

29

fish

Big **fish**, blue **fish**, little **fish**, mean **fish**, funny **fish**, fat **fish**, thin **fish**, flat **fish** – I love all **fish**. I sometimes wish I was a **fish**.

fish an animal that lives and breathes underwater

floor

Look! Somebody has left muddy footprints all over Nicole's mum's clean **floor**. Do you think it was Sparky the dog or Millie the cat?

floor the bottom of a room that people walk on

flowers

Hope has picked a big bunch of **flowers** for her mum for Mother's Day. Have you ever given someone **flowers** to say "I love you?"

flower the brightly coloured part of a plant that makes seeds

fly

This bird flies high in the sky. But did you know that some birds can't **fly**. Ostriches are too heavy to **fly** so they have to run very fast instead.

fly 1. to travel through the air
2. a type of insect

food

David's teacher said that they should eat healthy **food**. David didn't know that **food** could get sick! Can a doctor make **food** healthy again?

food things that can be eaten to provide the body with nutrition and energy

fork

Look at these delicious noodles. Some people eat noodles with a **fork**, and other people use chopsticks. Which would you use?

fork a tool with spikes at the end of a handle used for carrying food to the mouth when eating

friend

A **friend** likes spending time with you and comforts you when you're down. That's why your dog can be your best **friend** in the whole world.

friend a person (or animal) you know well and like a lot

frog

Most frogs are green, but this **frog** is bright red. I guess that's why it's called a tomato **frog**!

frog a type of animal that lives near water and has long back legs for jumping

front

Max is standing in **front** of Matt. Do you know the name of the boy who is standing in **front** of Max? He is in **front** of all the boys.

front a place that is further ahead than another place

fruit

Some people like bananas and melons and other yellow **fruit**. Other people like red **fruit** such as cherries. But I like **fruit** of every colour.

fruit the part of a plant that contains the seeds, often used as food

full

Natasha is carrying two shopping bags. One is **full** of heavy stuff and the other is **full** of light things. Can you tell which is which?

full contains as much as possible

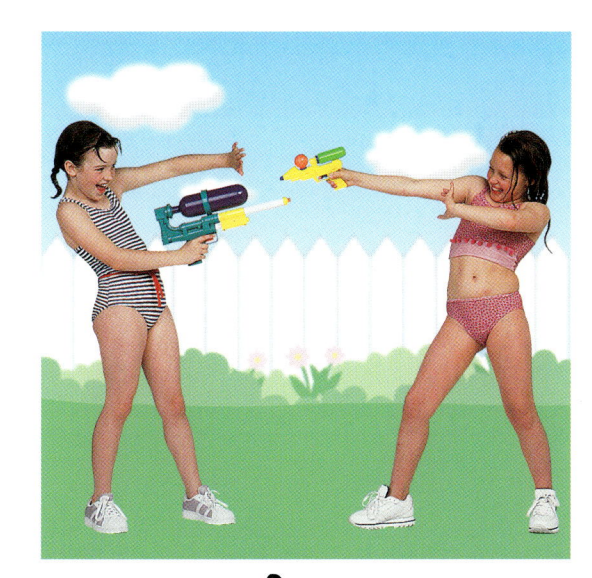

fun

It's so hot today that Natasha and Rebecca are squirting one another with water pistols. It looks like lots of **fun**, doesn't it?

fun enjoyable

Gg

game

"Simon's got the ball… but no, Michael's tackle was fantastic and he's got the ball back again. What a great **game** of football this is!"

game a fun activity with rules

gentle

Nicole is always **gentle** when she plays with Millie, but cats have very sharp claws. Nicole wishes that Millie would be **gentle**, too!

gentle calm and kind

ghost

Joe knows his sister, Grace, is frightened of the dark. That's why he has dressed up as a **ghost** to scare her. What a meanie!

ghost the spirit of a dead person

giraffe

A **giraffe** has a blue tongue. Its tongue is also rough and slimy – great for pulling leaves off trees, but not so nice to be licked by.

giraffe an African animal with long legs and a very long neck

girls

Here are some of the **girls** you've met so far in this book. Can you remember their names?

girl a female child

give

Eleanor and Holly are giving Jessica her birthday present. I love to **give** gifts to my friends when they have a birthday, don't you?

give to let someone have something

glass

These men are holding a piece of **glass**. Or are they? That's the thing about **glass**. It's see-through so it's hard to tell if it's there at all.

glass a see-through material that shatters easily when dropped

glasses

These are very smart new **glasses**. Now Heidi can see clearly. Without her **glasses**, everything looks a bit blurred.

glasses two lenses in a frame, worn over the eyes to help people to see better

glue

Emma is using **glue** to stick some pictures into a scrapbook. It looks like she's sticking more than just the pictures with that **glue**.

glue something used to stick two items together

go

The traffic lights turn green and the cars can **go**. Traffic lights have three colours – do you know what each one stands for?

go to move to a certain place

33

good

"Bring the ball, Sparky. **Good** dog. Now sit. **Good** dog."
Nicole is training her dog, Sparky, to fetch. **Good** girl.

good admirable and worthy of praise

grandfather

This is Nicole's **grandfather**. She calls him Grandpa and he calls her Nickel. Grandpa is Nicole's dad's dad. She loves Grandpa lots.

grandfather the father of your mother or father

grandmother

Nicole calls her **grandmother** Granny. Granny is Nicole's dad's mum. She is married to Grandpa. Nicole loves Granny lots, too.

grandmother the mother of your mother or father

grass

Look at these hills covered in fresh, green **grass**. If I were a sheep, I think these would be my favourite fields in the whole world.

grass a very common plant with thin green leaves

guess

Can you **guess** what's inside this box? No? Then I **guess** you need a clue. It's got eight legs…

guess to suggest something without knowing the answer

guitar

Matt is teaching Sam to play the **guitar**. That's a big **guitar** for such a little guy!

guitar a musical instrument with strings, played by moving the strings with your fingers and thumbs

Hh

hair

This gorilla has **hair** on its head just like you. But it has **hair** all over its body too. Imagine how long a **hair** cut would take if you were a gorilla!

hair the thin strands that cover your body, especially the top of your head

hamburger

Jake's mum has made him a giant **hamburger**. Can you see what it's got in it? What's your all-time favourite **hamburger**?

hamburger a round disk of mince, cooked and served in a bread roll

hand

Look at those **hand** prints on the wall. Who made them? Put your **hand** up if you did it – we'll soon see whose hands are covered in paint.

hand the part of the body at the end of your arm, that has a palm, four fingers and a thumb

happy

These are the things that make Tara **happy**: playing with a kitten, eating ice cream and pretending to be a princess. What makes you **happy**?

happy a pleasant or joyful feeling

35

hard

It's that little girl again. The big bed was too **hard**, the medium bed was too soft, but the little bed was just right and now she's gone to sleep.

hard very firm

hat

These people all wear a special kind of **hat** while they are at work. Can you work out what job each one does?

hat a covering for the head

head

Emma is standing on her **head**. Hope is also standing on her **head**, but Nicole is holding her legs and helping her to balance.

head the part of your body above the neck

hear

How do you know if there are two penguins hiding in your refrigerator? You can **hear** them whispering to one another.

hear to listen to sounds

heart

Your **heart** pumps the blood around your body. You can hear your **heart** beat if you listen through a stethoscope like this one.

heart the part of the body in your chest that pumps blood around the body

help

That's a big pile of books you've got there Sam. Whoops! I think you need some **help**. Here comes Matt. He'll **help** you.

help to assist

home

David has painted a picture of his **home**. He likes living in this house with his family. It's the place he feels most safe and comfy.

home the place where you live

horse

Before cars were invented, many people travelled by **horse**. How would you prefer to travel to school? By car or by **horse**?

horse a large domestic animal usually kept for riding

hot

David's mum is serving dinner. Careful! That pot has just come out of the oven and it's very **hot**.

hot high in temperature

hungry

David's dad said he was so **hungry** that he could eat a horse. I wonder what a **hungry** horse would eat? I expect it could eat a haystack.

hungry wanting food

hurry

Where is Lisa going in such a **hurry**? She's running over to talk to her friend Lauren. **Hurry**, Lisa, the school bell is about to ring.

hurry to move quickly

hurt

Oops! Emma has tied her laces together by mistake. She has tripped and landed on her knee. Ouch. That must have **hurt**.

hurt to cause pain

Ii

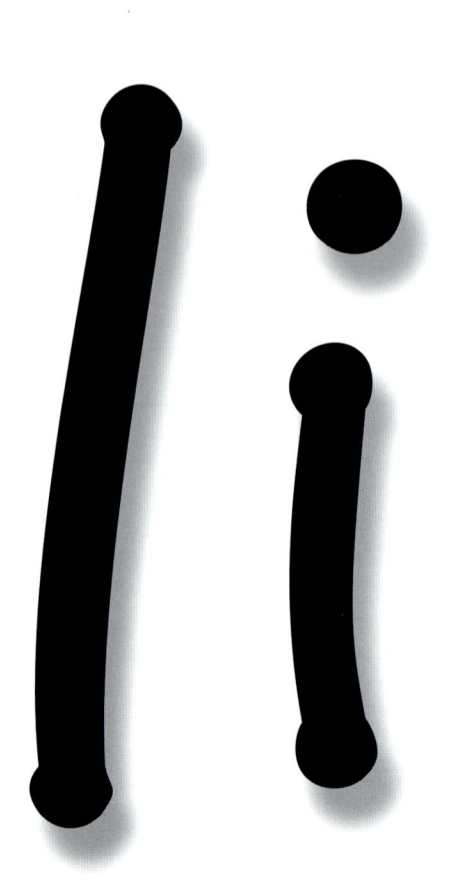

ice cream

This is Jake's favourite dessert: a big **ice cream** sundae, made with lots of different flavours of **ice cream**. Do you like **ice cream**, too?

ice cream a sweet, frozen food made from cream, sugar and eggs

inside

Jessica's aunt sent her a doll for her birthday. **Inside** the doll was another, smaller doll, and **inside** that was another doll and **inside** that...

inside within something else

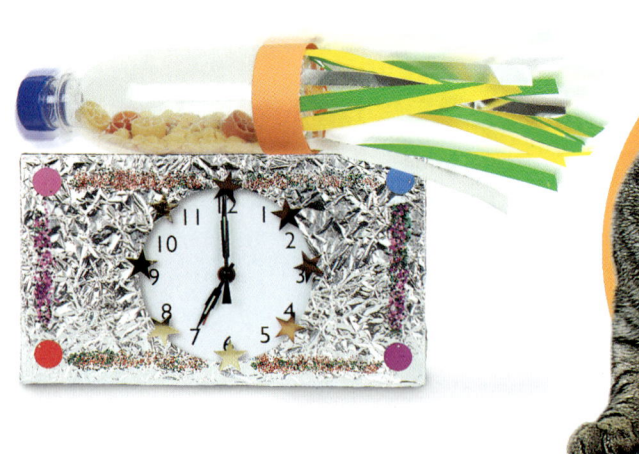

invention

Look at Maria's crazy **invention**. It's supposed to help her wake up in the morning. At 7 o'clock the rocket shakes loudly and makes a noise.

invention a new machine that somebody has just planned or made

itch

Nicole's cat, Millie, is scratching herself. She must have an **itch**. Maybe she has fleas. Oh no!

itch to feel that you want to scratch your skin

Jj

jacket

Scott is wearing his dad's **jacket**. Don't be silly, Scott. That **jacket** is much too big for you!

jacket a kind of short coat

jeans

Emma's mum wants to buy her a new pair of **jeans**, but Emma loves her worn out **jeans**. Which do you like best – new **jeans** or old **jeans**?

jeans trousers made from a tough cloth called denim

juice

Natasha and Rebecca are squeezing lemons. They will add ice, sugar and water to the **juice** to make lemonade. Mmmm, delicious.

juice the fluid inside fruit or vegetables that can be used to make a drink

jump

Jessica and her friends are playing Simon Says at her birthday party. "Simon says: **jump** in the air!"

jump to spring into the air suddenly

Kk

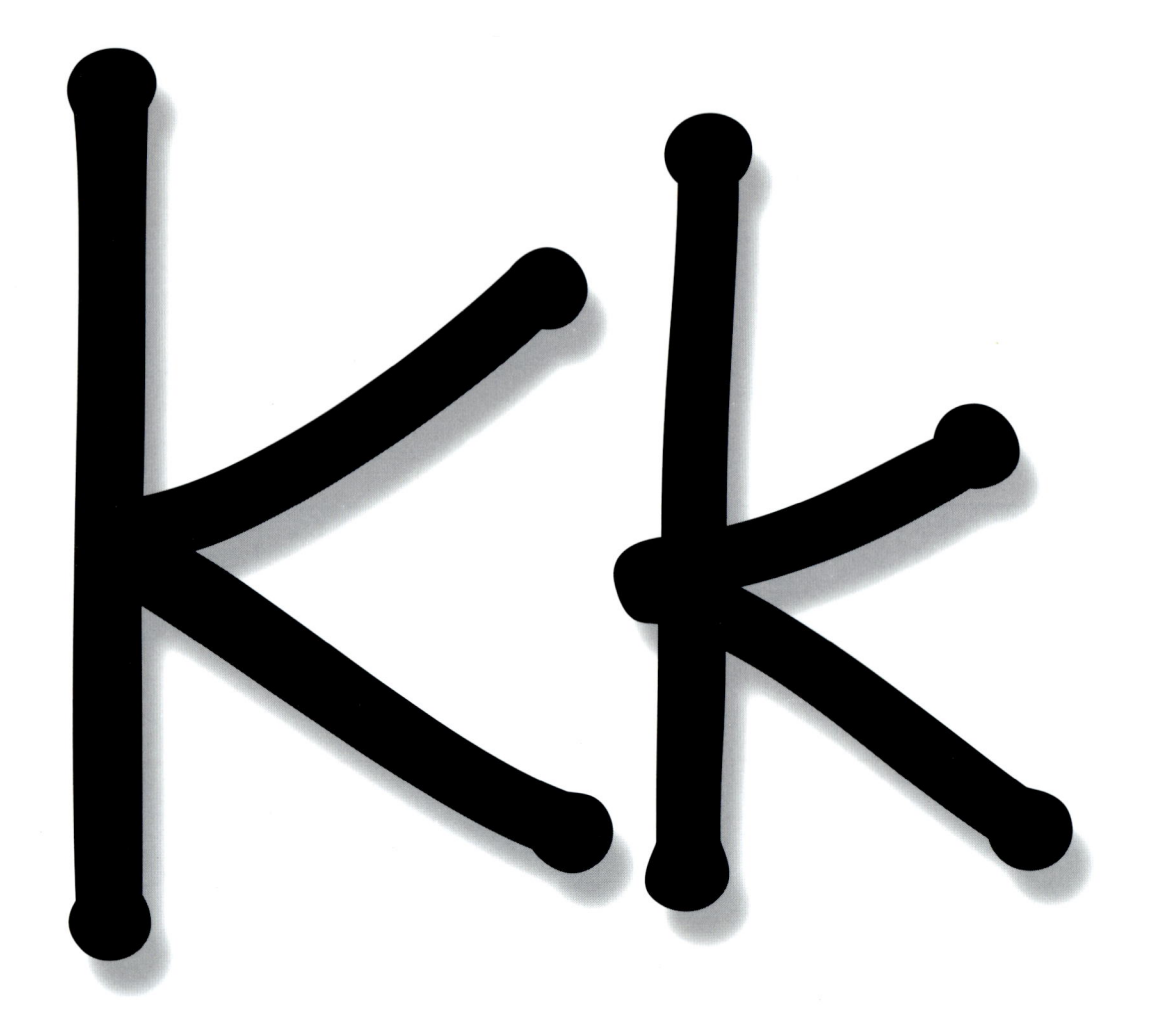

keep

Scott likes to **keep** all of his secret treasures in this box. Come on, Scott, show us what you **keep** in there.

keep to store something and not get rid of it

Old King Cole was a merry old soul,
And a merry old soul was he;
He called for his pipe,
He called for his bowl,
And he called for his fiddlers three.

kick

Sarah loves to play football. **Kick** the ball this way, Sarah. That's right, **kick** it hard. See if you can score a goal!

kick to hit something with your foot

kind

Hannah has given Claire her doll. That was **kind** of Hannah. Now Claire is giving her a big hug to say thank you. That's **kind** of Claire.

kind generous, caring and thoughtful

king

No wonder Old **King** Cole was merry. All he had to do was call out for anything he wanted. I wish I was a **king** too!

king a man who is head of a country

kiss

David hates it when his Aunt Sylvia gives him a **kiss**. She always leaves big smudges of lipstick on his cheeks.

kiss to touch with your lips as a sign of love

kite

It's a windy day – the perfect weather to fly a **kite**. Look at how this **kite** moves. It looks like it's dancing in the sky.

kite a toy that flies in the air and is attached by a long string held in someone's hand

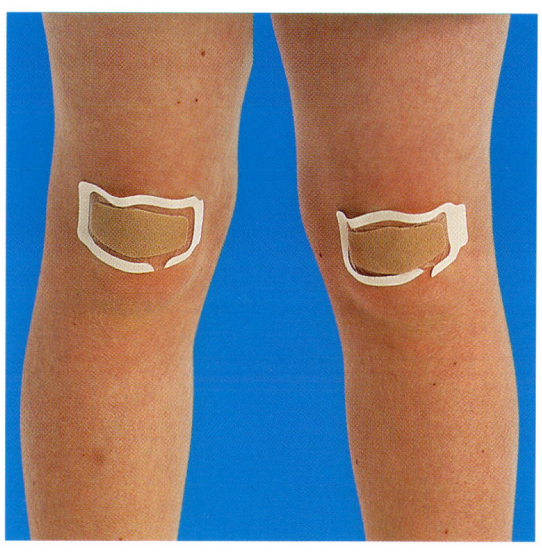

knees

Emma is often in such a hurry that she falls over and hurts her **knees**. That's why you will often see her with big plasters on her **knees**.

knee the joint between the upper and lower part of your leg that allows you to bend it

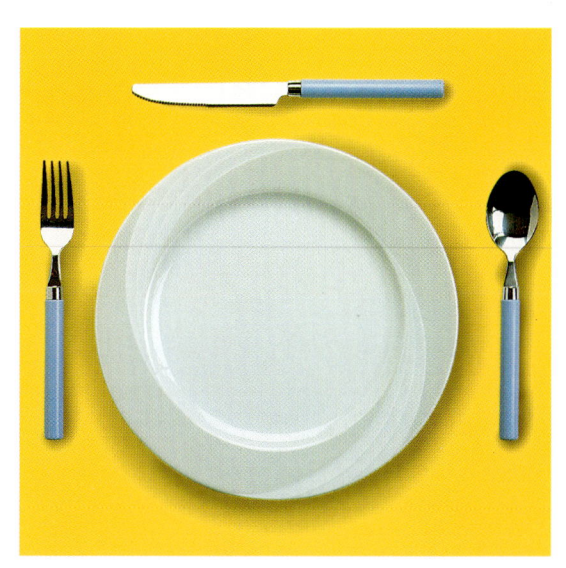

knife

Emma has set the table for dinner. But look at the **knife**. Do you think it is in the right place? Where would you have put the **knife**?

knife something you use to cut your food

know

Did you **know** that chameleons can change colour to scare off other chameleons? That's amazing, isn't it?

know to be certain of something

koala

This cuddly creature is called a **koala**. It comes from Australia. When it was a baby, this **koala** lived in its mother's pouch to keep it safe.

koala an animal from Australia that lives in trees and has grey fur

Ll

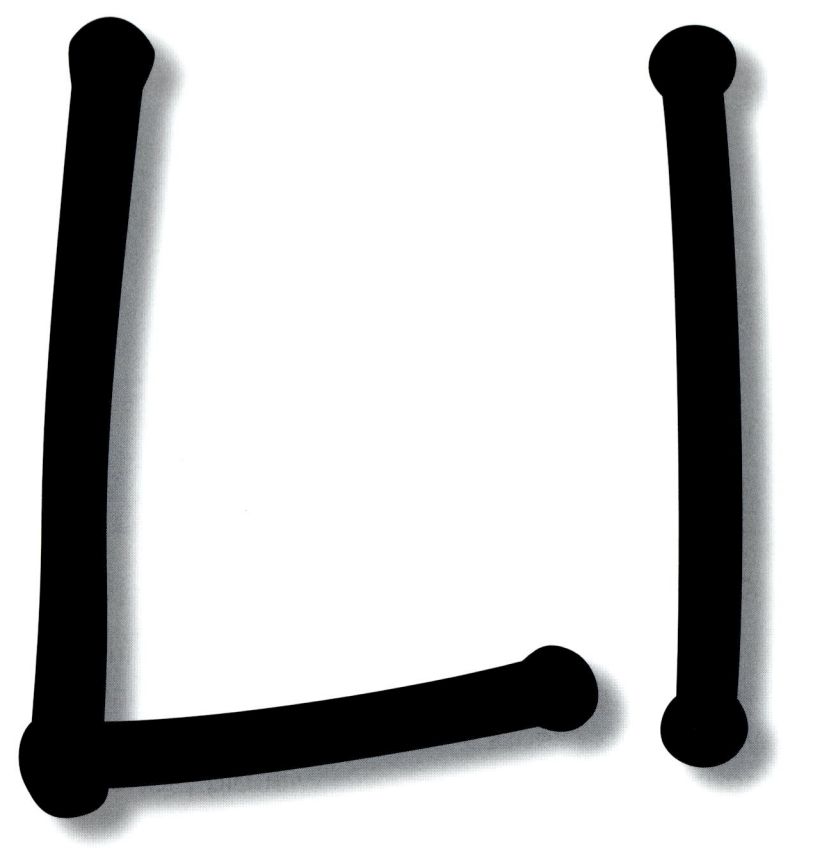

ladybirds

Did you know that there are girl and boy **ladybirds**? I wonder why boy **ladybirds** aren't called gentlemanbirds?

ladybird a type of insect that has black spots on a red or yellow body

last

When Jessica eats a piece of cake, she saves her favourite part, the icing, to eat **last**. Do you eat your favourite part first or **last**?

last something that comes after all the rest

laugh

Whenever Amy tells a joke, she starts to **laugh**. She laughs so hard she can't speak. Amy's **laugh** makes everybody else **laugh** too.

laugh the sound you make when you find something funny

leaves

In the autumn, the green **leaves** on trees change to yellow and orange. Then they all fall off and new green **leaves** grow back in the springtime.

leaves the usually flat green parts of a plant that are attached to stems or branches

left

Can you tell your **left** hand from your right? Here's a tip. Hold out both hands. On your **left** hand your fingers and thumb will form an L.

left 1. the side of your body where your heart is found 2. remaining

legs

Can you answer this riddle? Two **legs** sits on three **legs** and strokes four **legs**. Who do all these **legs** belong to?

legs 1. the lower part of your body, used for walking 2. the parts of an object that support it

light

It's a piggyback race! Luckily for Ellis, Katy is really **light**, so Ellis can run faster. Poor Rebecca – Natasha is not quite so **light**...

light 1. the opposite of heavy 2. the brightness that allows you to see things

lion

A male **lion** spends most of his time snoozing in the shade, while the female, called a lioness, works hard to hunt for food.

lion a large wild cat that lives in Africa or Asia

listen

Hope and her friends are playing hide and seek. **Listen** carefully, Hope, can you hear Lauren giggling? She will be easy to find!

listen to concentrate on hearing something

little

It's that **little** girl again! Which chair will she choose? Will she sit in the great big chair, the medium-sized chair or the **little** chair?

little 1. young 2. small

lizard

A **lizard** is a reptile. It hates to get cold. In fact, a **lizard** needs to sunbathe so it has enough energy to move.

lizard an animal with four legs, a long tail and scaly skin

long

Maria would like to have really **long** hair. She is wondering how **long** it would take to grow her hair down to her waist.

long 1. greater in length than usual
2. the opposite of short

lost

David **lost** his painting. He put it down for a few seconds and it disappeared. Oh no! It looks like he's just found it!

lost something that can't be found

love

Hope and her friend Rose **love** their pet rabbits. Aren't they sweet? You can see why Hope and Rose **love** them so much.

love to like someone or something very much

luck

Some people say that a black cat will bring you good **luck**. I think that's true. I'm very lucky to have such a cute little kitty cat.

luck good fortune

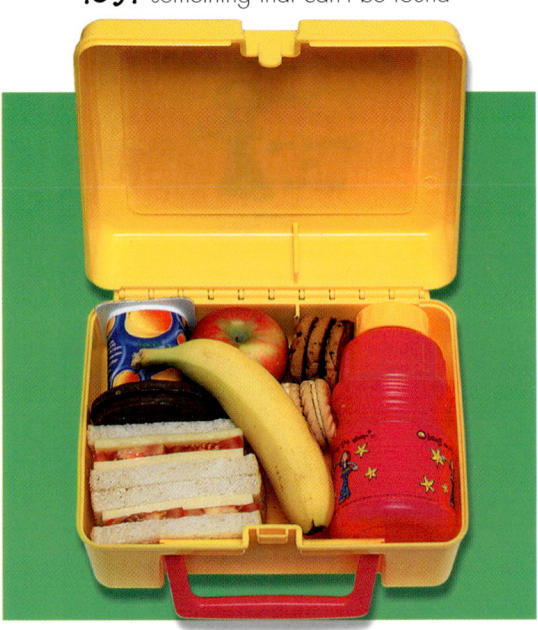

lunch

Jake's mum always gives him the best stuff in his lunchbox for school. Can you name everything Jake has for **lunch** today?

lunch a meal eaten in the middle of the day

Mm

magic

The magician at Jessica's party is doing some great **magic** tricks. Look, he has just made a rabbit come out of his hat.

magic a trick that makes something happen that seems impossible

make

Natasha is going to **make** a mask. She will **make** the face out of a paper plate and the hair out of coloured feathers.

make to create or build something

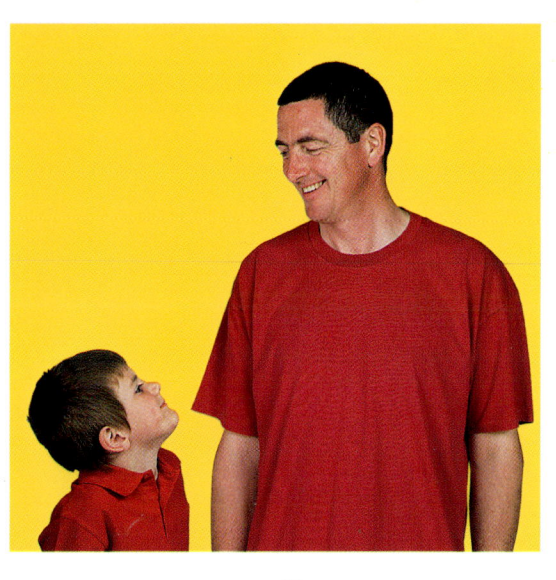

man

Sam is still a young boy, but when he grows up, he will be a **man**, just like his dad.

man a male grown-up

many

These children have been practising gymnastics. How **many** girls can stand on their heads by themselves? How **many** still need some help?

many 1. the number of 2. lots

45

medicine

Poor Abigail has a sore throat. Her mum is giving her some **medicine** to help her feel better.

medicine a liquid or a pill that you swallow to help cure an illness

middle

Jessica's friends have made a circle and asked Jessica to stand in the **middle**. Now they will all sing "Happy Birthday" to her.

middle the centre part

milk

David is wondering what has happened to his glass of **milk**. It was full just a minute ago. Who do you think drank it?

milk a healthy white drink that we get from dairy cows

mirror

Princess Pam always looks in the **mirror** before she goes out. She's making sure that her hair looks nice before she sees Prince Robert.

mirror an object made from glass that reflects things clearly

monkey

This **monkey** lives in a big group of family and friends. That way, some monkeys can search for food while others look out for danger.

monkey a small, furry animal with a long tail, that lives in trees

moon

Have you noticed how the **moon** seems to change shape? Sometimes it looks like a C and sometimes like an O. What will it be tonight?

moon a huge rock that circles the earth and reflects the sun's light at night

more

Are there **more** white flowers than yellow flowers? Why don't you count each kind to find out which there are **more** of.

more a larger amount of something

mother

Nicole, Lauren and James are sitting with their **mother**. Nicole and Lauren call their **mother**, Mum, but James is too young to call her anything!

mother your female parent

motorbike

This police officer rides a big **motorbike** so that he can get to the scene of a crime or an accident very quickly.

motorbike two wheeled vehicle powered by an engine

mouse

Some people are afraid when they see a **mouse**, but mice are usually harmless and I think they're cute. Spiders are another story!

mouse a small animal with sharp teeth and a long tail

mouth

A tiger has an enormous **mouth** lined with razor sharp teeth. This is one **mouth** that I don't want to get too close to!

mouth the part of your head that contains your lips, tongue and teeth

muddy

Look at these **muddy** boots and the mess they leave behind! I think these feet could belong to Rebecca, don't you?

muddy to be covered in soft, wet dirt

47

Nn

name

Do you remember the little girl who was trying out the different chairs? Have you guessed her **name** yet? Yes, you're right. It's Goldilocks!

name the word a person is known by

nest

A bird has used twigs to build this **nest.** Then it lined the **nest** with feathers to make a cosy place for its eggs to hatch.

nest the place where a bird lays its eggs

new

Hope's scooter is brand **new**. She loves it because it's so smart and shiny. It's great to get **new** things, isn't it?

new opposite of old

next

Tommy is stacking some blocks to make a tower. But look, he has decided to put a toy dinosaur on **next**. It's going to be a funny tower!

next something that comes right after something else

night

At **night**, I love to look up at the sky. I try to spot a falling star and make a wish on it. Sometimes you can see other planets at **night**!

night the time of darkness between sunset and sunrise

no

"I'll tidy up my room later. I want to go out and play now."
"**No**, you must do it now. I've asked you before. **No** more arguments."

no the opposite of yes, and a word used to disagree with something

noodles

Jake loves eating **noodles**. He tries to slurp up as many as he can in one try. Do you like slurping **noodles**, too?

noodle a long thin strip of pasta

nose

David's dad said that if he told a lie, his **nose** would grow bigger – just like Pinnochio. I wonder if that's true or if it's just another lie!

nose the part of your face below your eyes, used for smelling and breathing

now

At Jessica's party, they've eaten the cake, watched the magician and **now** it's time for the games to begin. Jessica wants them to start right **now**!

now 1. at this time
2. immediately

numbers

Here is a list of **numbers** from one to nine. Two of the **numbers** are in the wrong order. Can you see which ones are wrong?

number a symbol that represents how many of something there are

Oo

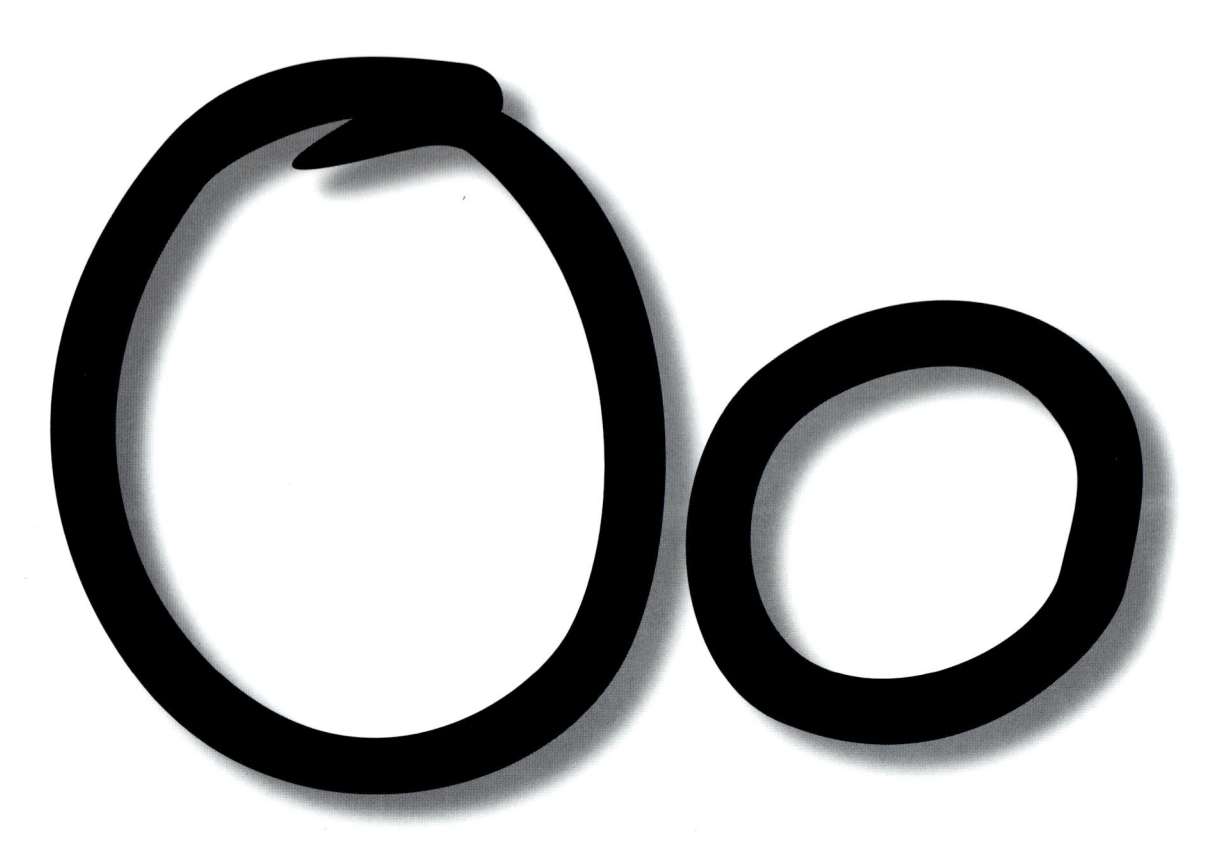

off

Ellis loves to jump **off** things. His favourite game is to climb on the garden wall and jump **off** again. Ellis is careful not to hurt himself.

off 1. away from
2. not on

old

This is Nicole's **old** teddy bear. Most of its fur has rubbed away, but Nicole still loves her **old** teddy and wouldn't part with it for anything.

old something that was made a long time ago

on

Natasha has finished making her mask and has put it **on**. Do you think she looks funny or scary with her mask **on**?

on 1. over the top of something
2. in use

onion

Hope's mum is crying, but she's not upset. She's just peeling an **onion** and that always makes her eyes sting and water.

onion a bulb with a strong smell used as a vegetable

open

That's strange. The door is **open** and I'm sure I closed it. Hang on, isn't that Lauren hiding behind the door? She must have opened it.

open not shut

opposite

What is the **opposite** of up? One truck has lifted the crate up in the air. The other truck has done the **opposite** – its crate is at the bottom.

opposite completely different from

oranges

Don't you love eating juicy **oranges**? Have you ever made silly faces with pieces of orange peel in your mouth?

orange a round reddish-yellow coloured fruit

out

Emma has taken everything **out** of her school bag so she can clean it. Have you ever seen so much stuff come **out** of one not-very-big bag?

out away from the inside of something

over

Natasha and Rebecca are playing leap frog. First, Natasha leaps **over** Rebecca, then Rebecca leaps **over** Natasha.

over above

owl

The **owl** hoots: "Who-who, who-who." I think he's asking someone a question. I wonder who-who?

owl a bird with a flat face and large eyes that hunts for food at night

Pp

paint

David's got some new paints. He seems to have every colour **paint** there is. He'll be able to **paint** even better pictures now!

paint 1. coloured substances that can be brushed onto a surface 2. to draw a picture using paint

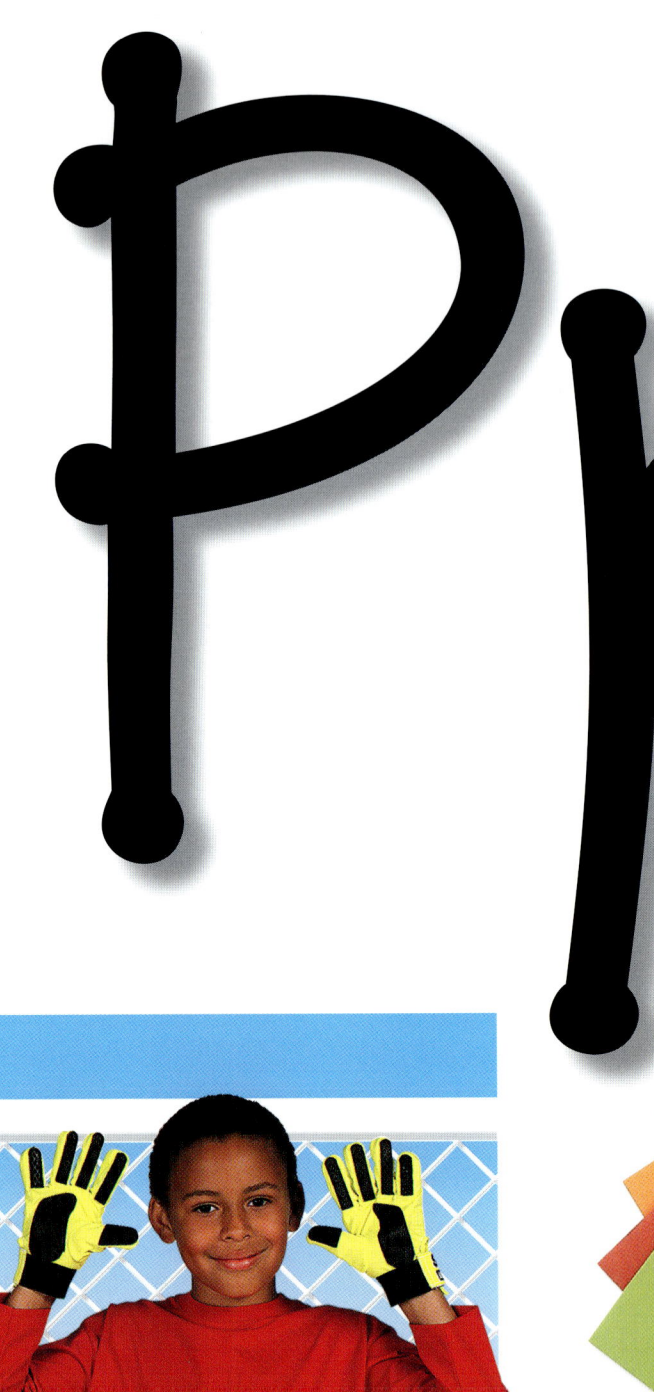

pair

Gareth is a goalkeeper. He is wearing his lucky **pair** of gloves. He never lets a single goal in when he wears these gloves.

pair two similar things that belong together

paper

Look at all of this pretty coloured **paper**. What would you do with it? Would you draw a picture on the **paper** or use it to make something?

paper a thin sheet of wood pulp, usually used for writing on

party

Jessica is taking lots of photographs at her birthday **party**. She is having such a good time that she wants to remember this **party** forever.

party a group of people gathered together to enjoy themselves

past

Zzzoommm! What was that? I heard a siren, but it shot **past** so quickly I couldn't really see. Did you see what went **past**?

past 1. beyond
2. a period of time that has already happened

peel

Hope's mum is trying to **peel** that apple very carefully, so that the skin she peels off doesn't break. Do you think she'll manage it?

peel to remove the skin of a fruit or vegetable

pen

David's **pen** is amazing. It has six different coloured inks in it. You just press a button and it writes in a different colour.

pen a long, round object filled with ink and used for writing

pencil

This is David's **pencil** case. It is filled with different coloured pencils and a **pencil** sharpener to keep the pencils nice and sharp.

pencil a long, round object with a sharp point used for writing or drawing

penguin

Here's a **penguin**, looking for its friends. Hey, I think I know where they may be hiding. Have you checked the refrigerator?

penguin a bird that lives in the Antarctic

people

All these **people** are watching you read this book. By the looks on their faces they seem to be enjoying themselves. Are you?

people human beings

perhaps

What should Princess Pam wear today? She could wear her royal purple dress, but **perhaps** her pink sparkly dress would be prettier?

perhaps maybe

photographs

Here are some of the **photographs** Jessica took with her new camera. These are the funny **photographs** that make her laugh.

photograph a picture made by exposing a film to light using a camera

picnic

It's a perfect day for a **picnic**, so Nicole and Lauren's mum has taken them on a trip to the country. Food tastes much nicer outdoors.

picnic a meal eaten outside

picture

David has painted a **picture** of himself. Do you think it looks much like him?

picture an image drawn or painted on paper, or a photograph

pie

Matt and Sam's dad has baked a perfect **pie** for lunch. Doesn't it look delicious?

pie meat, vegetables or fruit, surrounded by pastry and baked

piece

Sam's really hungry and can't wait to have some pie. What a big **piece** of pie for such a little guy!

piece a separate part of something

54

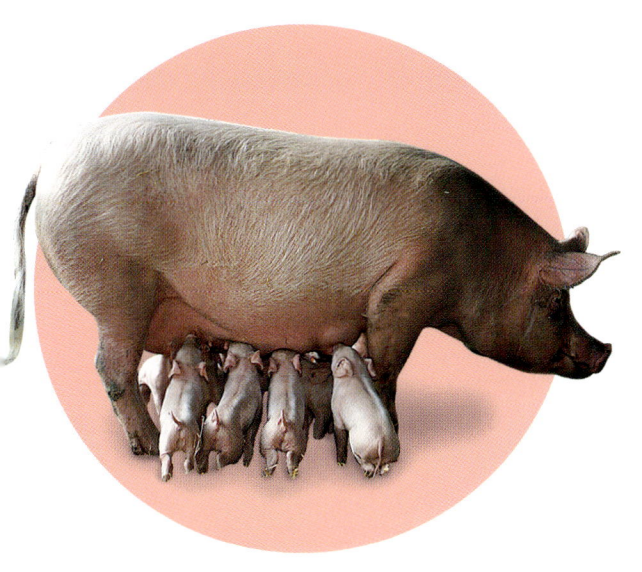

pig

A mother **pig** is called a sow and her babies are called piglets. These piglets are so greedy they'll soon be big pigs, like their mum.

pig a farm animal kept for meat

pirates

Nicole and Hope like to play make-believe games like "**pirates**". What games do you like to play with your friends?

pirate a sailor who steals other people's ships

pizza

Scott is going to have **pizza** for his dinner. His favourite **pizza** has pepperoni on it. What's your favourite **pizza** topping?

pizza a bread base covered in tomato, cheese and other toppings, then baked

plants

Matt and Sam are putting some **plants** into a window box for their mum. She loves **plants** so I think she'll like this window box.

plant a living thing which grows in the ground

plate

Look at this waiter balancing four plates of food. I'd like the **plate** of spaghetti, please. How about you?

plate a shallow dish used for serving food

police

I always feel safe when I see **police** officers because I know that nobody would dare to commit a crime in front of them.

police the people employed to make sure everybody keeps the law

A B C D E F G H I J K L M N O P Q R S T U V W X Y Z

popcorn

It's a real treat for Ellis to go to the cinema. Watching the film is fun, but eating the **popcorn** is even better.

popcorn grains of corn that have been heated until they pop open

potatoes

I love **potatoes**. Mash them, boil them, fry them, roast them, bake them – do whatever you like, just make sure I get enough **potatoes**!

potato a type of vegetable that grows underground

prickly

Imagine sitting on this **prickly** porcupine. Ouch! But that's exactly why a porcupine has prickles – so other animals leave it alone.

prickly something with lots of sharp points

pull

Who will win the tug of war? Come on everyone. All together now, one, two, three, **PULL**!

pull to make an effort to bring an object towards you

push

Lauren likes to **push** her little brother James in his pushchair. She likes going down hill but it's hard work to **push** him up hill.

push to make an effort to move an object away from you

puzzle

This **puzzle** is almost finished, there's just one more piece to go. I wonder if baby James could do this **puzzle** now. What do you think?

puzzle a game you have to solve

Qq

queen

Chloe likes to dress up and pretend she's a **queen**. Her friends think the game is boring. They think Chloe just likes to boss them around.

queen the female head of a country

question

David's teacher has asked him a really difficult **question**. He is thinking so hard about the answer his brain hurts.

question words asked in order to get an answer

quiet

Shhh, Lauren, you must be really **quiet**. Baby James has just gone to sleep and we mustn't wake him up.

quiet without making any sounds

quilt

Hope's granny made this beautiful patchwork **quilt** out of scraps of fabric. When Hope snuggles under the **quilt**, she thinks of her granny.

quilt a warm filling between two large sheets of cloth, sewn together and used as a bed covering

Rr

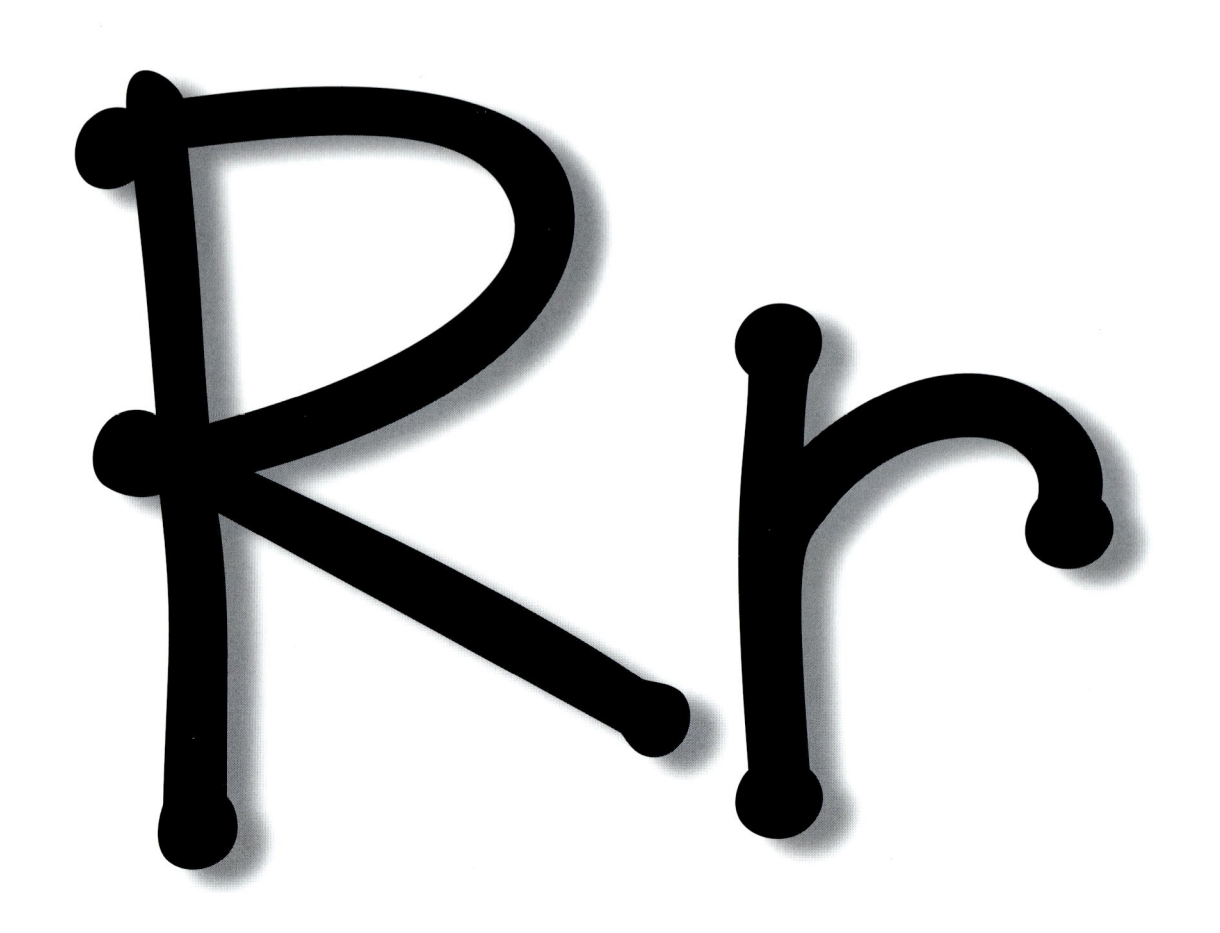

rabbit

A **rabbit** is a cute little animal with long ears, a funny, twitchy nose and big front teeth. Have you ever cuddled a fluffy **rabbit**?

rabbit a small animal that is good at digging with long ears and a short tail

race

Here comes Richard, running to the finishing line. Look! He's won the **race**. Richard is happy because he's never won a **race** before.

race a competition to see who can get to a point the fastest

rain

Alice loves the **rain**. Whenever it starts to **rain**, she grabs an umbrella and her rain boots and goes outside to dance in the puddles.

rain water falling from the sky in small drops

rainbow

Sometimes, if the sun shines at the same time as it is raining, a beautiful **rainbow** appears. Have you ever seen a **rainbow**?

rainbow an arc of different colours caused by the sun shining on raindrops

read

Grace is learning to **read**. She is starting off with a book with lots of pictures and not too many words. Do you know how to **read** yet?

read to understand written or printed words

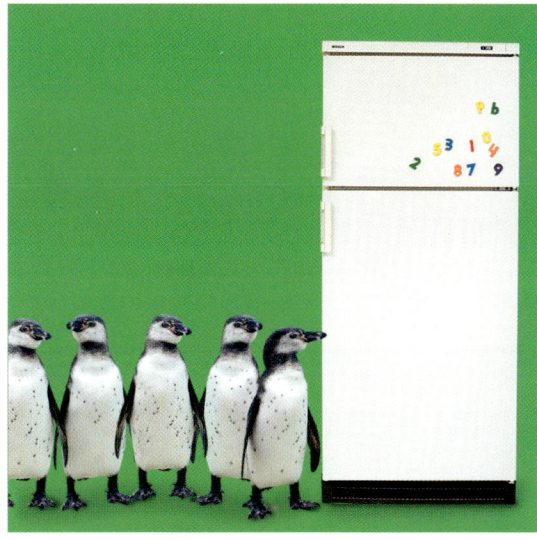

refrigerator

Here are more penguins queuing up to get in the **refrigerator**. It's a bit strange, I thought you kept food in a **refrigerator**, not penguins.

refrigerator a cabinet for keeping food and drink cold

remember

Here's a game to test your memory. Look at this picture for one minute. Then close the book. Can you **remember** what things you saw?

remember to bring into your mind a fact you already knew

rhinoceros

A **rhinoceros** is a big, powerful animal. But do you know what a **rhinoceros** eats to make it so big? Just lots of grass and leaves.

rhinoceros a large plant-eating animal with thick skin from Africa or Asia

ride

Jessica's party is over so now she can go for a **ride** on her new bicycle. She feels like she could **ride** far, far away.

ride to sit on something and move it about

right

Rebecca uses her **right** hand to play tennis, and Natasha uses her left hand. Which hand do you use most – your **right** or left?

right 1. the side of your body that is away from your heart 2. correct

river

From high in the sky, this **river** looks like a shiny snake, winding its way through the countryside.

river a large amount of water flowing along a natural path

rock

Max can't shift that **rock**. I think he will have to build his camp around it. Never mind, it will make a great shelter for one side.

rock a large stone

rockets

The huge **rockets** attached to this space shuttle will blast it into outer space. Have you ever wanted to travel into space?

rocket a device that burns fuel to push itself forward very fast

rooms

Rose's beautiful doll's house has five **rooms** in it. How many **rooms** are there in your home?

room an area in a building divided off with walls and a door

rough

Can you tell what this **rough** surface is? It's the skin of a pineapple. It's odd, because most fruit has quite smooth skin.

rough not smooth

run

It's sports day. These children will **run** to the end of the field, touch a post, and then **run** back again. I wonder who will **run** the fastest?

run using your legs to move very quickly

Ss

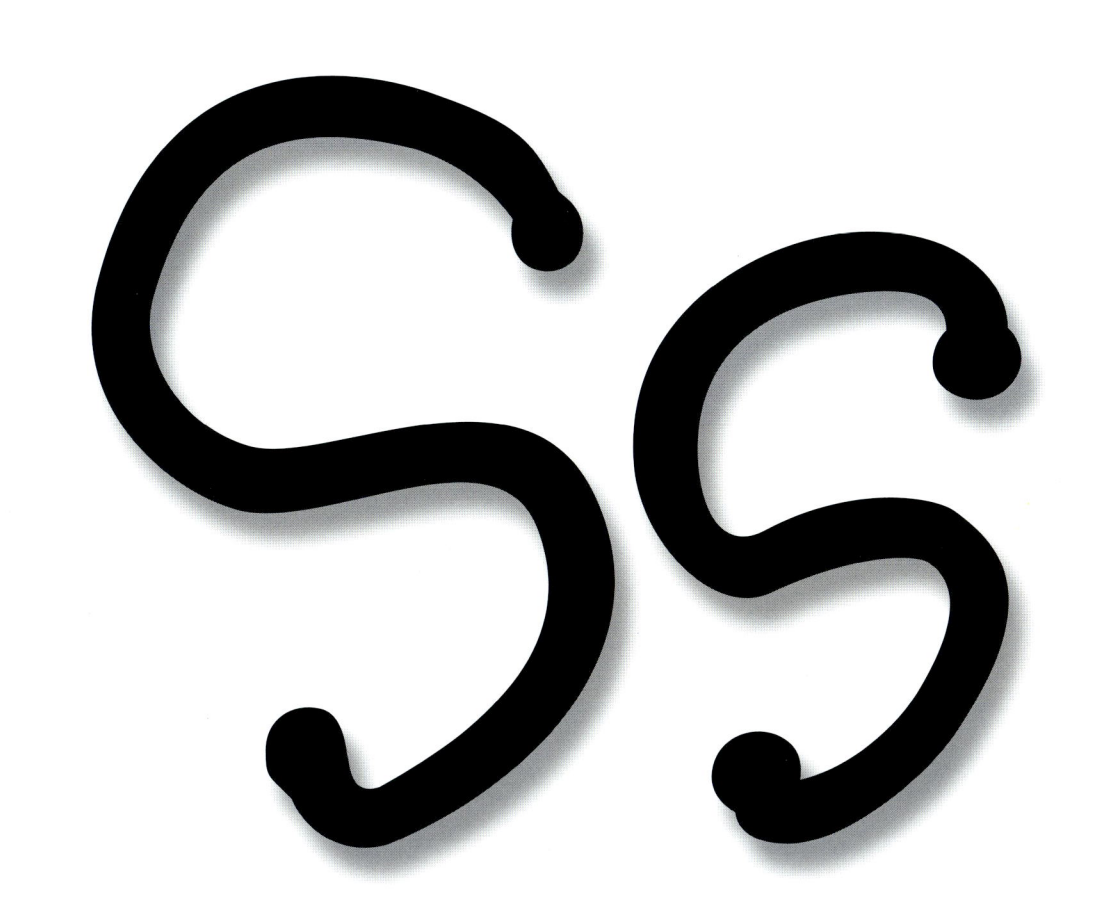

sad

Jessica is feeling **sad**. Her party is over and all of her friends have gone home. Cheer up Jessica, it's Eleanor's birthday party next week.

sad feeling unhappy

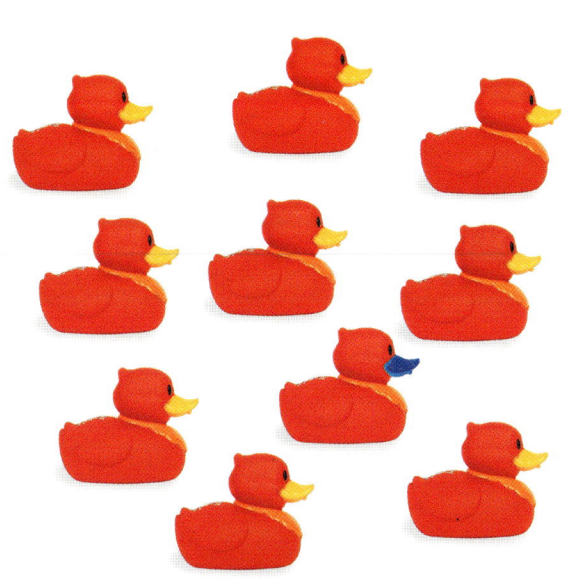

same

All of these ducks look the **same**, don't they? Have another look. Can you spot the duck which is not the **same** as the others?

same identical

sand

Nicole and Lauren are playing in the **sand**. They're trying to build ten sandcastles in a row. Do you think they'll manage it?

sand tiny grains of rock found on the seashore

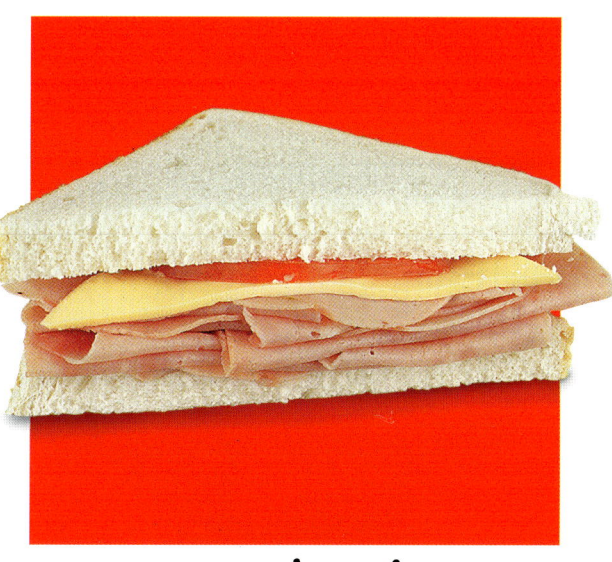

sandwich

Whenever David eats a **sandwich**, he wonders if the first **sandwich** had sand in it instead of good things such as ham, cheese and tomato.

sandwich a filling between two slices of bread

scared

"Oh Granny, those big, sharp teeth of yours are making me **scared**!" "Come a little closer, there's nothing to be **scared** of," said the wolf.

scared frightened

school

It's Sam's first day at **school** today. His friend Grace starts **school** today too. Have you started **school** yet?

school a place where children are taught

scissors

At school, Sam and Grace cut out shapes with **scissors**. They use special **scissors** with rounded ends so they can't hurt themselves.

scissors two blades joined together and used for cutting paper

see

Julia and Rose are playing "I Spy". They can **see** shampoo, scissors and a shark. What can you **see** that begins with an "s"?

see to look with the eyes

shampoo

Max is washing his hair, but he has used too much **shampoo**. Look at all that foam. Careful, Max, **shampoo** can sting if it gets in your eyes.

shampoo a liquid soap for washing hair

shapes

Do you know the names of these **shapes**? I can see a circle, a heart and a triangle. What other **shapes** are there here?

shape the pattern an object's outline makes

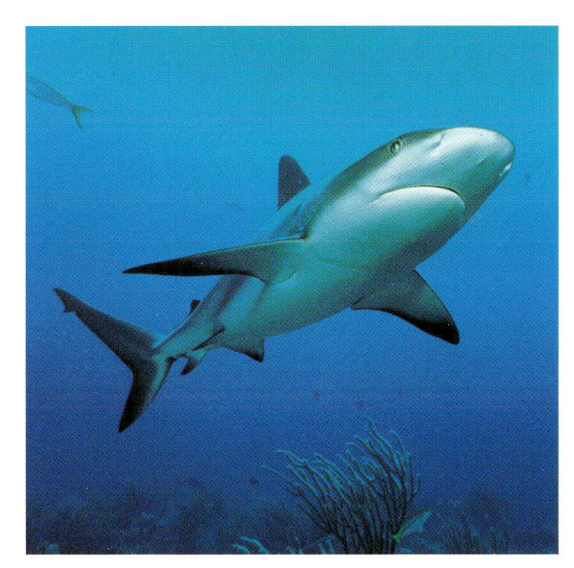

sharks

I love looking at **sharks** in an aquarium because they are so fast and beautiful. I don't think I'd like to meet a shark in the sea though!

shark a dangerous creature that lives in the sea or in an aquarium

sheep

This **sheep** has a thick coat to keep it warm in the winter. In the spring, its coat is cut off. The wool makes clothes to keep us warm in winter.

sheep a farm animal with a thick coat, kept for its meat and wool

shell

Have you ever held a **shell** up to your ear? It sounds as if you are listening to the crashing waves of the sea.

shell the hard, protective covering of an animal

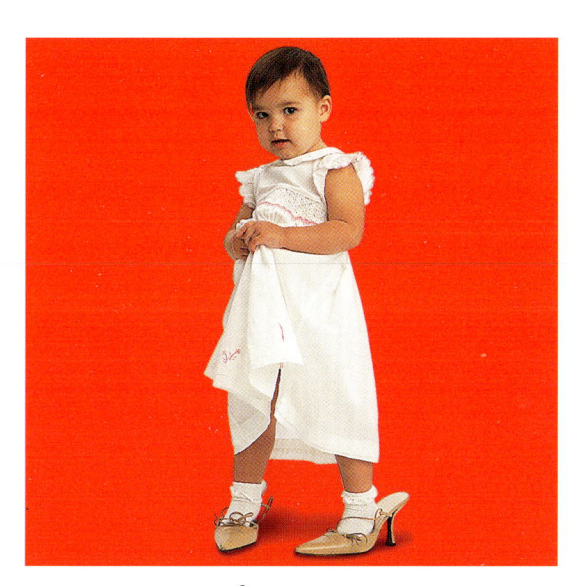

shoes

Are those your **shoes**, Katy? What's that? They will be your **shoes** when you're grown up? You will need to grow quite a bit before they will fit!

shoe a strong covering for the foot often made from leather, plastic or canvas

short

Rose is **short** and her Uncle John is tall. Uncle John can reach things from a high shelf, but Rose is much better at hiding in small spaces.

short not as tall as usual

shout

Scott is watching his favourite football team play. He can **shout** louder than anyone else at the game. "Go the Bolton Blues!"

shout to call loudly

shut

Quick! **Shut** that box! I think something scary is trying to escape from it.

shut move an opening to close it

shy

Grace is very **shy**. Whenever she meets someone new, she tries to hide her face away and she blushes bright pink.

shy nervous when you are with other people

sick

Poor Chris is feeling **sick**. He has a headache and a sore throat. Why don't you go to bed, Chris? I'm sure you'll feel better in the morning.

sick feeling unwell or as if you want to vomit

silly

When her sister is upset, Olivia pulls **silly** faces until her sister laughs. What sort of **silly** face would you make to cheer up someone?

silly foolish or childish behaviour

sing

These children are learning to **sing** a new song. They will **sing** in front of their class on Friday. Can you **sing** any songs?

sing to make music with your voice

sisters

Nicole and Lauren are **sisters**. Sometimes they quarrel, but most of the time they get on well. I've always wanted a sister. How about you?

sister a girl who has the same parents as you

sit

It's time to listen to a story. Everyone gather round and **sit** down quietly. Lauren, why don't you **sit** on that pink chair?

sit to rest on your bottom

skateboard

Matt is a real whizz on his **skateboard**. He can do quite a few clever tricks on it. I wish I could ride a **skateboard** as well as Matt does.

skateboard a narrow board on wheels

skip

Do you know how to **skip**? It's difficult at first, but when you know how, you won't want to stop.

skip to jump or hop over a rope

skirt

Hope is deciding which **skirt** to wear today. Do you think she should chose the red **skirt** or the white **skirt**?

skirt a piece of material fastened around the waist

sky

If you look up into the **sky**, you can see a lot of different things: birds, clouds, kites. What is Rose looking at in the **sky**?

sky the air high above you if you look up

sleep

There is nothing that a cat likes better than to snuggle up somewhere warm and go to **sleep**. A cat will **sleep** all day if you let it.

sleep the time when you are resting very deeply, usually at night

slow

This **slow** tortoise plods around the garden looking for lettuce to eat. It can't move fast with that heavy shell, so it's lucky lettuce can't run away!

slow taking a longer time than is usual

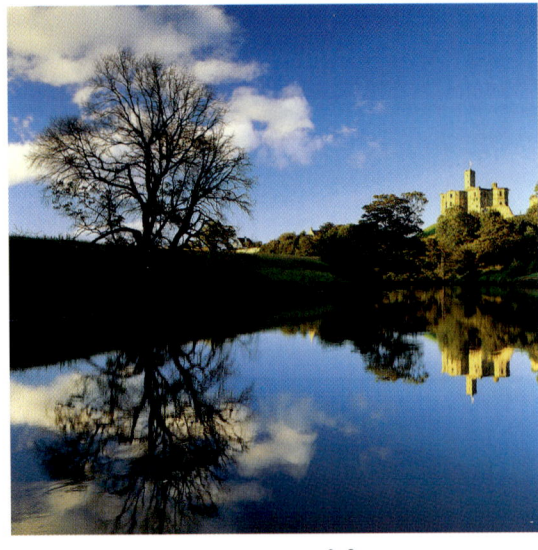

smooth

This lake is as **smooth** and still as a mirror. In fact, you can see the tree and the castle reflected in it, just like a real mirror.

smooth an even surface with no bumps or roughness

snake

This **snake** eats mice and other small animals. It wraps itself around its prey and squeeeeezes hard. Then it swallows its food.

snake a long, narrow animal with no legs and a dry, scaly skin

sneeze

a-a-a-tish-oo!

A-a-a-TISH-oo! In summer, pollen from flowers tickles some people's noses and makes them **sneeze** a lot.

sneeze when air is blown out of the nose suddenly, with no control

snow

In some countries, **snow** falls in winter. Everything gets covered in a thick, icy-white blanket of **snow** and children have snowball fights.

snow the frozen water that falls from the sky in soft, white flakes

soap

Emma has been playing in the garden and now her hands are dirty. She is using **soap** and water to get them clean again.

soap a bar or liquid used to clean away dirt

socks

Here are lots of **socks**: green **socks**, orange **socks**, blue **socks**, spotty **socks**, stripy **socks**, stinky **socks**. Just how many **socks** are there?

sock a piece of soft material shaped to go over the foot

soft

Look at these ducklings. They are covered in **soft**, fluffy feathers called down. Have you ever touched a duckling's **soft**, little body?

soft not hard

spider

When a big **spider** sat down beside Miss Muffet, she got a huge fright. Would you be frightened if a **spider** sat next to you?

spider a small animal with eight legs

spoon

Jake is eating his ice cream with a long-handled **spoon** so he can reach the bottom of the glass. Have you ever used a **spoon** like that?

spoon a small bowl with a handle, used for lifting food to the mouth

squirrel

This cheeky **squirrel** appears in my garden whenever I put out nuts. It munches them all up, then disappears with a whisk of its bushy tail.

squirrel an animal with red or grey fur and a long, bushy tail that lives in trees

stars

Jessica had this dress for her birthday. It is covered in little gold **stars**. She has even got matching socks with **stars** on them.

star 1. a shape with five or more points sticking out
2. a far-away sun, seen as a point of light

67

strawberries

Lots of juicy, red **strawberries** tell me that summer has arrived. I love **strawberries**. What is your favourite kind of fruit?

strawberry a small sweet red fruit with seeds on the outside

strong

Billy and Joe are so **strong**. Look at them carrying that big piece of wood. Do you think you would be **strong** enough to lift it?

strong powerful

sugar

What a delicious-looking bowl of fruit. Fresh, juicy strawberries taste great, but if you sprinkle them with **sugar** they are even better.

sugar tiny, very sweet grains sometimes added to food or drinks

summer

In the **summer**, the weather is warm and the days are long. It's a great time of year to go to the beach. Do you like the beach in **summer**?

summer the warmest season of the year

sun

The **sun** is shining down on Hope at the beach. She is wearing a **sun** hat and sunscreen to stop the **sun** burning her skin.

sun the star that gives our planet heat and light

swim

There's nothing better on a hot day than going for a **swim**. Have you ever worn a snorkel and mask to see what's underwater?

swim to move through the water using your arms and legs without touching the bottom

Tt

table

This **table** is just the right height for children. After eating their dinner, these children will use the **table** for painting and making things.

table a piece of furniture which has a flat surface supported by legs

take

Lauren is trying to **take** the teddy from Nicole. Lauren wants to have a picnic in the garden, but Nicole doesn't want her bear to get dirty.

take to remove from a place

talk

Builders have to **talk** on the phone to organise their work.
"Hello, I'd like to order a thousand nails and a new hammer please."

talk speak

tall

How **tall** are you? These boys are both the same age, but one is **tall** and one is short. They are both great at football though.

tall 1. the height of something
2. higher than usual

teacher

This is Sam's **teacher**, Mrs Ward. She is kind and friendly and knows the answers to all of Sam's questions. Isn't she clever?

teacher a person whose job it is to explain facts to children

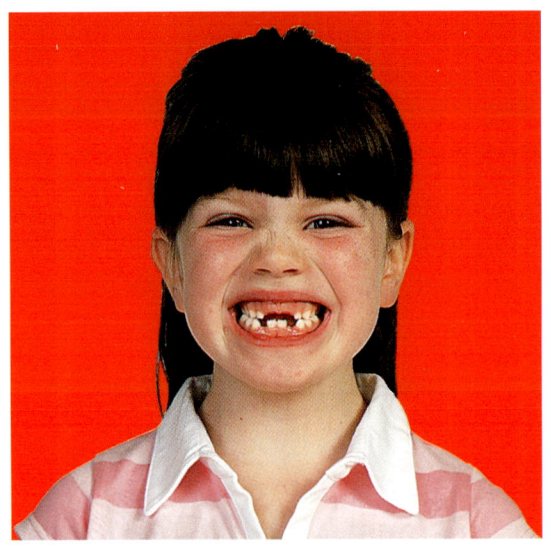

teeth

Hope's two front baby **teeth** have fallen out. She'll soon have adult **teeth**. But until then, thee'll thound thlightly thtrange when thee thpeakth.

teeth the hard white objects in your gums

telephone

The **telephone** is ringing. I wonder who it is. What do you talk about to your friends on the **telephone**?

telephone a machine which allows you to talk to people who are in a different place

television

Max's mum says that he can watch **television** for one hour every day. He spends ages trying to decide which programmes to watch.

television a machine that can pick up and show broadcasts of moving pictures and sounds

tent

When Matt and Sam go camping with their parents, they share this little **tent**. It's a good thing Sam's such a little guy, isn't it?

tent a portable shelter made from material spread over poles and fastened to the ground

then

Emma was so sleepy she put on her socks and shoes first, and **then** she tried to pull on her jeans. Of course, her feet got stuck!

then after that

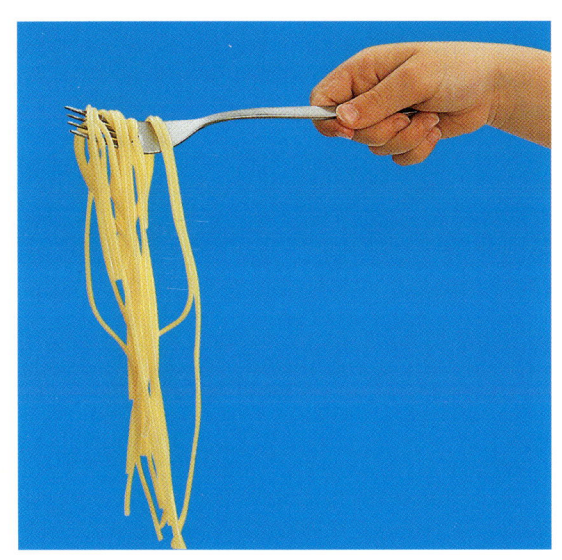

thin

Spaghetti is long and **thin** and smooth. Have you ever slurped a strand into your mouth and pretended you are eating a worm?

thin something much longer than it is wide

thirsty

There's nothing better than a long cold drink when you're **thirsty**. I love drinking juice with lots of ice cubes bumping against my lips.

thirsty wanting something to drink

this

Do you know what **this** is? I'll give you a clue. You can find **this** animal at the end of **this** book.

this the one referred to here

throw

Steve loves to play catch. He is trying to **throw** and catch the ball 20 times using only one hand. Do you think he'll do it?

throw to send something travelling through the air

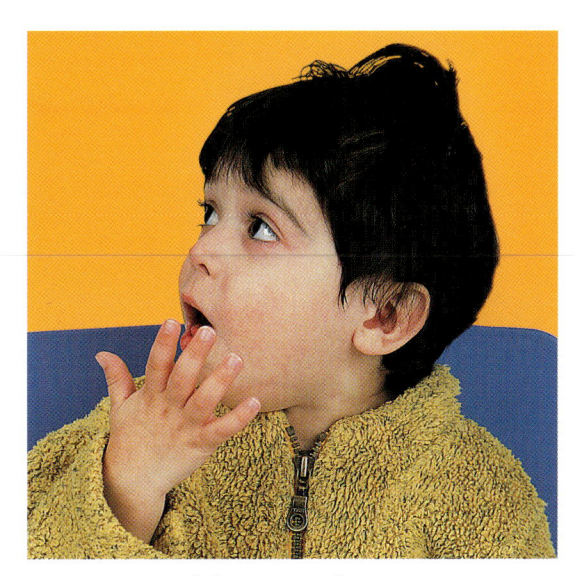

thunder

Dylan doesn't like the noise of **thunder**. He knows that **thunder** can't hurt him, so he is trying to be brave. Usually he runs and hides!

thunder the deep rumbling noise heard after lightning

tickle

Harry loves to **tickle** Lizzie. Lizzie loves it too, even though being tickled makes her laugh so much her tummy hurts.

tickle to touch somebody so the tingling feeling makes them laugh

tiger

Look at this **tiger**. He is the biggest wild cat of all. A **tiger** isn't scared of water and will sometimes go swimming to catch tasty fish to eat.

tiger a large wild cat with orange and black stripes that lives in Asia

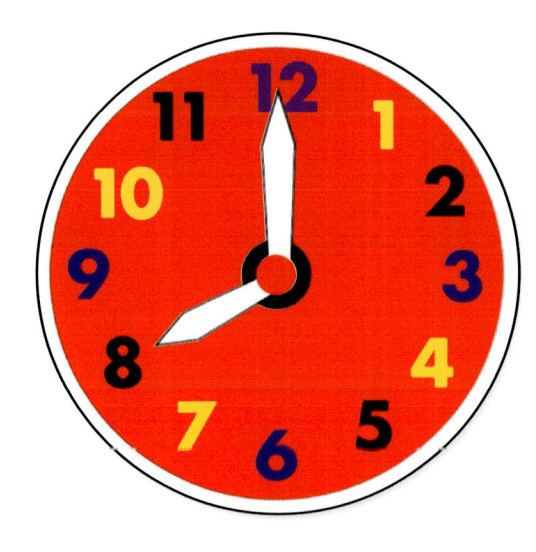

time

The big hand of the clock is pointing to 12 and the little hand is pointing to 8. The **time** is 8 o'clock. Can you tell the **time** yet?

time a particular point in the day, measured in hours and minutes

tired

Today was Sam's first day at school. It was lots of fun, but now he's very **tired**.

tired feeling exhausted and needing to sleep

tomorrow

Tomorrow Sam will be off to school again. He'd better go to bed early tonight so he'll be ready for another busy day **tomorrow**.

tomorrow the day after today

toothbrush

Do you use a **toothbrush** and toothpaste to clean your teeth every morning and night? What colour is your **toothbrush**?

toothbrush a small brush on a long handle used to clean the teeth

top

Climbing up to the **top** of the slide is worth it for the fun of sliding down to the bottom again.

top the highest point

tractor

A **tractor** is very useful on farms. It can pull a plough and haul heavy loads. I wonder how farmers managed before they had tractors?

tractor a farm vehicle with large back wheels used for pulling heavy loads

train

This is a passenger **train**, taking people from city to city. I love travelling by **train** and watching the countryside whizz past.

train carriages or wagons joined together and pulled by an engine along tracks

treasure

A princess always has lots of **treasure**. Princess Pam has crowns, jewellery, coins and precious stones. She keeps her **treasure** very safe.

treasure money and precious jewels

tree

Look at this big **tree**. It's hard to believe that it started off as a tiny seed, no bigger than your thumb.

tree a tall, long-living plant with a trunk, branches and leaves

truck

This huge **truck** carries heavy loads between towns. Have you seen a **truck** like this before?

truck a motor vehicle used to carry goods

T-shirt

I love this **T-shirt** because it's got lots of hearts on it. Do you have a favourite **T-shirt** and if you do, why do you like it so much?

T-shirt a short-sleeved top without any buttons

Uu

umbrella

It's raining, but Sam is staying nice and dry under his **umbrella**. That's a big **umbrella** for such a little guy.

umbrella material over a frame and attached to a long handle, used to protect against the rain

uncle

This is Nicole's **uncle** with her dad. They are brothers. Do you think they look alike? Would you guess they are brothers?

uncle the brother of your father or mother

under

Heather and Mel are pretending it is raining. They are sheltering **under** the table. When they pretend there is a flood, they sit on top of the table.

under below

up

Hope has climbed **up** this steep hill, so that she can whizz down on her scooter. But now that she's **up**, she's almost too tired to go down.

up 1. to move to a higher place
2. in a higher position

Vv

vacuum cleaner

Amy's toy **vacuum cleaner** doesn't clean the floor as well as a real **vacuum cleaner**, but it does have a nice friendly face.

vacuum cleaner a machine that sucks up dirt from carpets

vase

Hope picked some beautiful flowers from the garden. Her mum has put them in a **vase** with some water to make them last as long as possible.

vase a jar for holding flowers

vegetables

Look at these delicious fresh **vegetables**. My favourite **vegetables** are potatoes and peas. Which **vegetables** do you like to eat?

vegetable the part of a plant that can be eaten

very

These boots are **very** big. Scott can fit his hands as well as his feet into the boots. But that's a **very** odd way of wearing boots.

very extremely

75

Ww

walk

Hope is supposed to be taking Tiggy for a **walk**. But if you ask me, Tiggy is the one who is taking Hope for a **walk**!

walk to move on foot at an ordinary pace

want

When Connor grows up he wants to be a famous hockey player. What do you **want** to be when you grow up?

want to wish for something

wash

Poor Grace has fallen over in the mud. She wasn't hurt, but she did get dirty. **Wash** your face, Grace. Then **wash** your knees, please.

wash to clean with soap and water

watch

Emma is buying a **watch** to stop her from being late all the time. She can't decide which **watch** she likes best. Which one would you choose?

watch a small clock on a strap worn on the wrist

water

Natasha and Rebecca have been playing with **water** pistols. Now they are both completely soaked. Even their shoes are full of **water**!

water a clear, tasteless liquid essential for life

way

Maria and Max have got lost in a maze. They don't know which **way** to turn. Can you help them to find their **way** out?

way 1. the direction
2. the path

wheels

A bicycle has two **wheels**, a tricycle has three **wheels** and a car has four **wheels**. Is there a vehicle here that has got more than four **wheels**?

wheel a circular object with a rod through its centre, allowing it to turn

where

Matt and Sam have lost their ball. They've looked all over for it, but they can't see **where** it has got to. **Where** can it be? Can you see it?

where in what place?

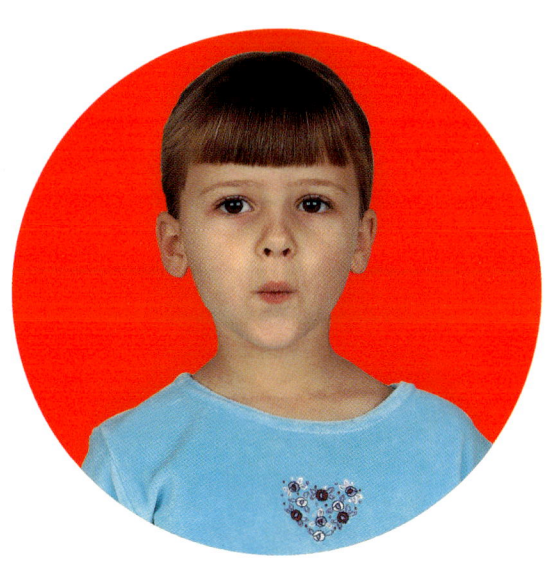

whistle

Lizzie can **whistle** without any problem, but when I make my mouth into a circle and blow, no sound comes out at all.

whistle to make a noise by blowing through your lips

wind

What a storm! The rain is lashing down and the **wind** is too strong to walk in. I wouldn't like to be out in this weather, would you?

wind a current of moving air

window

Maria loves looking out of her bedroom **window** at the big tree growing just outside. What can you see from your bedroom **window**?

window a sheet of glass set into a wall allowing people to see in and out

winter

When **winter** comes and the weather grows colder, the leaves fall off the trees and everywhere looks very bare.

winter the coldest season of the year

wish

If you ever see a falling star, you should make a **wish**. But keep your **wish** a secret, otherwise it may not come true.

wish something you want a lot

woman

Hope is still a young girl. When she grows up, she is going to be a **woman**, like her mum.

woman a female grown-up

wood

Scott is collecting **wood** for his dad to make a fire. It's a heavy load, I hope he doesn't drop it all!

wood the trunk of a tree, usually after it has been cut down and used

write

Grace can't really **write** properly yet, but she does know how to **write** her name. How about you? Can you **write** your name yet?

write to mark words on a surface

78

Xx

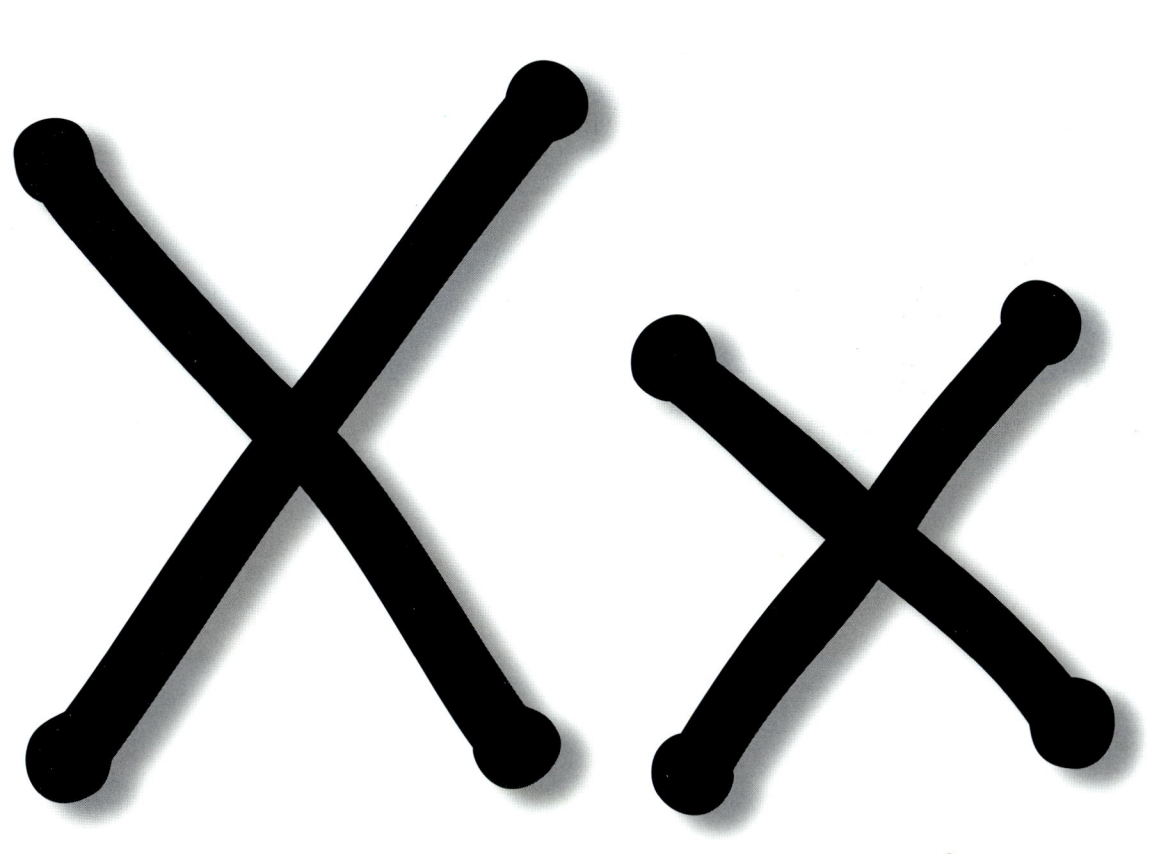

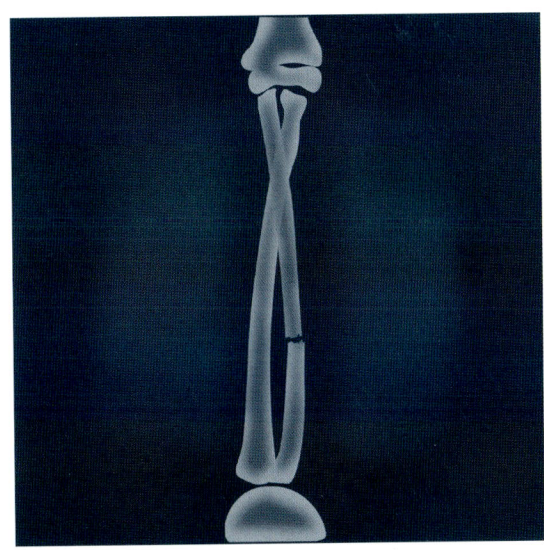

X-ray

This is an **X-ray** of Emma's broken arm. An **X-ray** is a photograph of your insides. They help doctors to see how to make people better again.

X-ray a picture made by passing radiation through the body so the bones show up

xylophone

It's not too difficult to play a pretty tune on a **xylophone**. Have you ever tried to make music by banging on a **xylophone**?

xylophone a musical instrument made of wooden bars that are hit with hammers

Yy

yawn

What a big **yawn**! Karen is very tired after a long day and wants to go to bed. Good night, Karen. Sleep well.

yawn to take in a deep breath and let it out again because you are tired

yes

"I've tidied my room. Can I go out to play now?"
"Your room is very tidy, well done. **Yes**, you may go out now."

yes a word used to agree with something

yesterday

Do you know the names of the days of the week and what order they come in? If **yesterday** was Monday, then what day is it today?

yesterday the day before today

young

Nicole is **young**, but not as **young** as her sister Lauren, and Lauren is not as **young** as their baby brother. He's the youngest of them all.

young having lived for a short time

Zz

zebra

A **zebra** may look like a kind of stripy horse, but I wouldn't try to ride one if I were you!

zebra a type of wild horse with black and white stripes that lives in Africa

zigzag

Did you know that if you write a whole lot of joined-up zeds in a line, you can make a **zigzag** pattern? Try it yourself.

zigzag a path that changes direction sharply several times

zip

Emma's favourite top has a **zip** down the front. Emma usually finds her **zip** easier than buttons. But what's gone wrong here?

zip a fastener which works by moving a tab between two rows of small teeth

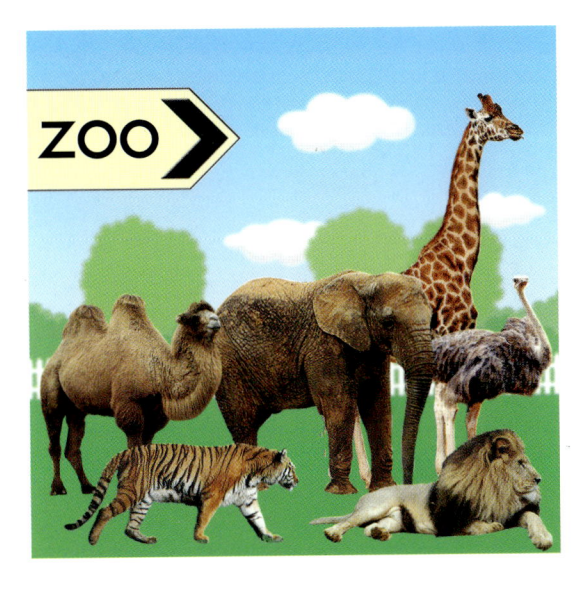

zoo

A **zoo** is a place where you can see lots of different animals. Do you know the names of these animals? Have you ever seen them in a **zoo**?

zoo a place where unusual animals can be seen

Aa	Bb	Cc	Dd	Ee
Ff	Gg	Hh	Ii Jj	Kk
Ll	Mm	Nn	Oo	Pp
Qq	Rr	Ss	Tt	Uu
Vv	Ww	Xx	Yy	Zz